UnLoading THE OVERLOAD

A CHRISTIAN GUIDE TO MANAGING STRESS

Cliff Powell
and
Graham Barker

Gazelle
BOOKS

Originally published 1998 by Strand Publishing, Sydney, Australia, *Unloading the Overload: Stress Management for Christians*

This revised edition first published 1999 by
Gazelle Books, Concorde House, Grenville Place,
Mill Hill, London NW7 3SA, UK.

ISBN 1 899746 17 X

Cartoons by Michael Head.

Designed and produced for the publisher by
Gazelle Creative Productions
Concorde House, Grenville Place, Mill Hill, London NW7 3SA.

Contents

Foreword

There are many books out on the stress of modern day life, and many are helpful. There are also many books out on developing your spiritual life, and many of these are helpful as well. What is unique about this book, and what it does well, is tie together the experience of stress in everyday life with the depth and well-being of our life before God.

Too often the psychological profession falls prey to giving only 'techniques' for dealing with the experience of being overwhelmed. While these are helpful, what we ultimately need is to become people who do not get into the position of needing one more technique.

What we need is transformation. We need to be changed into people who face life from a different position. Instead of being 'stressed', we need to be changed into people who 'stress life' itself! We need to be putting the pressure of the Light onto whatever outside circumstance we find.

In this book, Cliff and Graham tell us how to do that by changing into people of love, light and truth. They tell us how to orientate ourselves according to the model of Jesus, the wisdom of Kingdom living and the findings of contemporary psychology. In this way we can transcend much of the stress of life in the world.

I enjoyed *Unloading the Overload*, and I recommend it for spiritual growth, refocusing and finding a different approach to modern day living.

Henry Cloud, PhD
Author of Boundaries

To
William Potter Powell,
who drank a full cup of life's pain, stress and overload;
who evidenced the effects of that in his body;
but who kept his gaze firmly fixed on God, and by
prayer, perseverance, service and humility
touched many lives.

And to
Frank McInnes
Pastor, mentor, friend.

Introduction

Much of Western civilisation is disease-ridden, and one of our worst diseases is hyperactivity. Interestingly, in clinical textbooks, hyperactivity is a disease of childhood. We need to do some growing up!

At every level of society people report being overwhelmed by the pressures they face. Much of the time it is work stress. A lot of people have not seen much of that wonderful commodity called Increased Leisure Time that was so confidently predicted twenty-five years ago. Professional people and small business owners are two groups who generally report increased stress because of increased work demands.

Someone has accurately commented that many of us in society are only two pay-packets away from financial disaster. With no savings, and no reserves because most of the pay packet goes into rent and other repayments, many folk are just scraping through. If we were to lose our job tomorrow, chances are the car, the large-screen TV and a few other items would be repossessed. And we would have to look for new accommodation. So financially we are not in great shape. It is another area of overload, threatening to overwhelm us at any time.

Add relationship stresses to the picture. As clinical psychologists, we constantly work with people who are overloaded by pressures coming from relationships that are just not working. Somewhere in the rush towards the Great Technological Nirvana, it seems Western society has lost its moorings in the area of people-relating. Loneliness, your name is overload, too.

We are both committed Christians, with a special interest in the landscape of evangelical Protestants. And boy, are we in trouble! Somewhere back in the time of the Reformation, when our forebears were busy tossing everything overboard that they could not find in the Bible, they threw out some basics that *were* there but that had not been well recognised in Scripture. Somehow they made the mistake of thinking that activity was sanctified by God but rest was not. They did a pretty good job of snuffing out the contemplative life. Away with cloisters and meditation and spiritual exercises! Here we were at last, *getting serious* for God. In Protestant churches the mad spiral of hyper-activity reached new heights. We got into raising clouds of dust for God. We hoped he would be impressed!

The young man was dropping out of the ordained ministry. He had served just one year in a church. Completely disillusioned, he shared a not uncommon story – excitement, dreams and hopes gradually eroded by unrealistic expectations, unreal demands, a loss of confidence in his suitability for ministry and, finally, an inability to cope. 'I think I just made a mistake,' he said. 'I should never have gone into the ministry. I never realised the load I'd be under, and now I know that I can't take it.'

I (Cliff) had been a lecturer involved in the training of this young man. He had tons of potential. His resignation was a loss to the ministry.

But the grinding, overwhelming pressure is not confined to local church leaders. Have you ever looked into the eyes of some of your local or national leaders? Have you, like both of us, sensed the tiredness, felt a taste of what they carry sweep across you, even as they pour themselves out on the next urgent task? In most cases they do a magnificent job, but too often they leave before their time with minor health problems, heart attacks, depression, burnout. The accumulated effect of over-load.

The tragedy in church, family and personal life is even more widespread. How many lay Christians discover each year that they just cannot cope because the load is too great? Sometimes under medical advice, sometimes because it is just good common sense, they resign positions, pull back or completely quit.

The church scene is a mirror of the way our present society, both secular and Christian, operates. You sure don't need to be a churchgoer to feel overloaded! Basically, as a society we are hyperactive. And we are slow to attend to the things we need to do to change.

This tendency to overload is the focus of our book. We share a conviction that this is not how it should be. We do not have a 'rose-tinted glasses' view that life should not have tough times, setbacks, health problems or difficulties. After all, to borrow Larry Crabb's phrase, we are all 'living outside the Garden'.

Nor do we believe that in the grand scheme of things Christians should have it easier. Following Jesus is not an invitation to attend some kind of divine Club Med holiday resort. The Christian who is doing nothing for God has at least as big a problem as the Christian who is doing too much. There is a cross to be taken up, and that sure must mean something!

What we do have is a conviction that far too often we are overloaded in life because we are tackling things in ways that are not in our, or God's, best interests. We create a lot of the pressures that threaten to destroy us. We set ourselves up for overload. We overemphasise being busy and doing things for God. We do not spend enough time checking out *his* agenda.

Unloading the Overload is written for people who feel overloaded. Along with a different understanding of living, it aims to provide some realistic, achievable action-steps so that changes can be made. It is not a quick-fix recipe book, but we believe there is something here for everyone who feels the load is too great.

Unloading the Overload is unashamedly based on Scripture, and it builds from our convictions as Christians. If that's too heavy for where you're coming from, it may not be the book for you (although you could try replacing the Christian emphasis with a more vague 'need-to-attend-to-the-spiritual-foundations' type of thinking!). But the truth is we think overload is fundamentally a spiritual problem, and we just could not get too far into looking at it without asking ourselves: How did Jesus cope with the incredible task facing him, in the midst of a non-comprehending environment? So we have built from Scripture in sizeable chunks. Obviously, we have also integrated research findings from psychology and some case studies from our clinical experience where these add to the picture.

The book is divided into sections. **Part One** emphasises practical steps that relate to handling the *external* demands and pressures that come to each of us. It is as though every day has a certain height 'wall' of busy-ness and stress that we have to clamber over. These are the external demands. This section looks at ways we can go about reducing the height of the wall, or putting stress-reducing bricks into the wall, so that it's not such a tough climb. We look at the benefits of prioritising, setting limits, sharing the load with others, developing a network of supportive friends, and attending to exercise and diet.

Part Two focuses on *internal* changes that we can make. Even if we cannot make changes to the wall of external circumstances and thus reduce its height, we can work inwardly, strengthening our capacity to handle walls of this size. Inward changes, if we can make them, enable us to climb better and jump higher. This section includes guidance on how we can better view ourselves, change our inner experiencing, and learn to incorporate relaxation techniques into our living.

The final chapter begins an integration of these two areas, looking at the central importance of establishing a life-rhythm that emulates the rhythm that God has implanted in his world. It involves making a new priority to create time to rest, allowing our spirits to reach out to God in renewal during these times.

Chapters are broken into a number of sections. 'Foundations' sections seek to lay a knowledge base for the aspect under consideration. 'Review' sections are designed to help you personalise the material and begin the process of unloading the overload. We want to help you make changes that will be beneficial. The questions in these sections can also be the basis for sharing with others in small groups who are committed to helping each other find less stressful patterns of living. Finally, in some chapters we have included specific 'Action' sections to give you additional help in building the content of that chapter into some positive change for yourself.

Throughout the book, to help illustrate points, we refer to overloaded people that we have worked with in our clinic. In all cases, names have been changed so that the people involved are incognito, but the truth of their situation has been accurately described.

If you have no problem in the area of being overloaded or overwhelmed, save yourself money and time. But if, like us, you struggle with how to control your world before it controls you, then this book should help.

Cliff Powell
Graham Barker

Part 1

Handling your
external world or
Reducing the height
of 'the Wall'!

Chapter One
Choosing Priorities

Foundations

Carl Jung is reputed to have said once, 'The world will ask you who you are, and if you do not know, the world will tell you'. The point he was making, of course, was that there are so many demands in our world competing for our time and attention that they will consume us completely without our having any say at all, unless we set our own priorities. Unless we deliberately reflect on what we want to do with our lives, we will, at some point, simply find ourselves looking back with regret. Others will have set the complete agenda for our life.

One of the qualities that marks people as different from the mineral, vegetable and animal kingdoms is that we can choose priorities for our lives and pursue them.[1] We are not simply at the mercy of our drives, our instinctive urges, our biological programming. We are not determined by the accumulation of experiences and forces acting upon us. We act upon our environment and shape it, as well as having it act upon and influence us. As humans we have the capacity to plan ahead, to delay gratification, to put our needs aside, to feel for others and to sacrifice now in order to benefit later.

It is this distinctive capacity that has enabled artists, musicians, poets, engineers, communicators, theologians, athletes, surgeons, scientists, leaders and people from every sphere of human endeavour to become outstanding in their field. They have chosen priorities in life and given themselves to achieving these. They have not been content to let the world tell them who they are.

John Goddard was such a person.

The story is told that when John was fifteen years old he overheard his grandmother and aunt complain about the fact that during their lives they had missed out on doing lots of things they would have liked to do. He made a decision, then and there, not to let his life drift by without achieving the goals he wanted to set. He wrote out for himself a list of 127 goals.

Goddard set as life priorities a tremendous variety of experiences. He decided, for example, that he would

- explore ten rivers
- climb seventeen mountains
- have a career in medicine
- visit every country in the world
- fly an aeroplane
- retrace the travels of Marco Polo
- read the Bible from cover to cover
- read the works of Shakespeare, Aristotle, Dickens, Plato and a dozen other great authors
- become an Eagle Scout
- dive in a submarine
- learn to play the flute and the violin
- attend a church mission
- marry and have children
- read the entire *Encyclopaedia Britannica*

Twenty-five years later, at the age of forty, Goddard had already achieved 103 of his 127 goals, including being married with five children! There was no way that he was prepared to let himself drift through life.[2]

Goddard may be an extreme example of someone determined not to waste the life that was his. It is even possible he was a bit extreme in his determination to choose his way through life, rather than drift through.

However, the point is a crucial one. Unless *we* do the work of thinking things through and weighing up priorities, we are in great danger of having the rest of the world dictate how we will spend our time and what we will give our energy to. And being caught in that trap is one surefire way to rapidly become overloaded.

Having a Sense of Control

Many studies from the field of psychology have confirmed the importance of having a sense of control in our lives. Much of the anxiety, stress and sense of overload that people carry comes directly from the fact that they feel things have got out of control in their lives.

Hobfoll, in his 1988 book *The Ecology of Stress*, suggested that stress comes from the perception that our life feels overloaded. We experience the perception that the demands around us threaten the resources that we have – our status, our position in the community, our financial stability, our relationships, our home or our possessions – with the result that we experience a sense of overload.

For example, one famous study, carried out by American psychologists D.C. Glass and J.E. Singer,[3] exposed two groups of subjects to a loud, extremely unpleasant noise. The subjects in one group were told they could stop the noise by pressing a button, but they were requested not to do so unless absolutely necessary. The subjects in the other group had no button to press at all.

Jesus was not prepared to let life dictate to him how he would live.

In running the experiment, none of the subjects who had a button to press to eliminate the noise actually used their button, so both groups actually experienced exactly the same exposure to noise. Even so, when they were asked to perform a series of problem-solving tasks after exposure to the noise, the group who had the button *and who therefore had a sense of being in control of the noise* did significantly better on the task than the group with no sense of control.

The relevance of studies such as this to our sense of overload is obvious. *Taking the time to think through our priorities brings a sense of increased control to our life.* When we fail to prioritise, we put ourselves in the situation of trying to live primarily to meet the demands and expectations of others, of being under the control of others. When we feel out of control we inevitably feel overloaded.

Did Jesus Set Priorities?

You do not have to look far in the Gospel records before you discover that Jesus was a person who set priorities. He was not prepared to let life dictate to him how he would live. Instead, he *chose* the methods and goals towards which he would work.

Jesus' Priority in Methodology

The account of the temptations of Jesus can be looked at from a number of angles, each providing useful guidance for our lives. However, many commentators see this incident as primarily being about methodology.

At his baptism Jesus receives his Father's anointing to begin the ministry for which he has come. The Holy Spirit comes upon him in the form of a dove, and his Father commends him before the people. Now, driven by the Spirit into the desert, he must work through his methodology. *How* will he be the Messiah?

Will he try to win a following by being a bread-supplier, someone dedicated first of all to meeting people's needs in order to share the good news about the Father's love with them? Or will he try to get a following by being a miracle-worker, doing tricks like jumping from the temple spire? The crowds will surely flock after him if he does, and then he can share the good news with them. Or should he bow down to Satan, use the

Enemy's tactics to get a following, be a military conqueror who will gain control of all the world's kingdoms so he can share his message with them?

In each case he rejects the temptation to use this approach.

Certainly, out of compassion he will at times feed the hungry crowds. And at times, in response to human need, he will work miracles. But neither of these will be his primary method. Somewhere in the resolution of the temptations there is the affirmation that he will take the way of the Suffering Servant. He will come preaching the good news, using the methodology of love, being ready to lay down his life.

Jesus chose, as a priority, *how* he would carry out his ministry. He was not prepared to use violence. He was not prepared to 'take it as it comes' or 'go with the flow'. He was not prepared to let others dictate to him how he would act. Some commentators believe that Judas' betrayal was really an attempt to force Jesus into a corner where the only thing he could reasonably do would be to defend himself, and thus begin the revolution against Rome. Jesus refused to be backed into any such corners. Instead, he chose to affirm the priority of his methodology, to love instead of retaliate, to lay down his life, and so to accomplish his Father's purposes in providing salvation for the world.

Jesus set priorities and chose where to devote his energies from day-to-day.

Jesus' methodology at this point stands in contrast to the approach of the religious leaders around him. They are prepared to be expedient; he is not. They are prepared to be violent; he is not. They claim to be about God's business, but they use ungodly methods. John records for us that they decided to have Jesus put to death: '... it is expedient for us that one man should die for the people, and not that the whole nation should perish' (John 11:50, NKJV).

Recently a man came to our clinic seeking advice on how to rebuild his marriage. His wife had only just left him, taking the children with her. He was not handling the situation very well, and his job was now also under threat. His wife had told him that she was no longer prepared to put up with his frightening anger outbursts – periods of rage when he would be completely out of control, screaming abuse at her and the children, usually over some quite trivial incident. All his life he had used intense anger as a method for getting control over people around him in order to get his own way.

Faced with the task of learning about himself, and especially of growing up in his handling of anger, he quit therapy. He found it easier, as some do, to hide behind spiritual-sounding phrases such as 'She's not obeying God's word' and 'Women are supposed to be submissive, and she's not doing that'. Putting the problem on her was easier than facing his own brokenness and learning to change. What he had to learn was that using anger to control others is a pretty useless methodology for relationships. Not learning it cost him his marriage, his family and his career.

Relationships flourish only when there is a methodology of love.

So we see Jesus, at the outset of his ministry, giving priority to his methodology, to *how* he will work. He will only do what is godly.

Establishing a clear sense of God-endorsed methodology in our activity is profoundly wise in terms of heading off overload. Self-focused methods, approaches aimed at engineering people into the Kingdom of God, putting our sole emphasis on *doing* for God – all of these risk taking us into territory that will ultimately overload our resources.

Jesus' Priority in Long-Range Goals

There are many clear statements made by Jesus about his long-range goals. But perhaps none is clearer than his statement to his disciples after finding them preoccupied about earthly posts of importance: 'The Son of Man came not to be served, but to serve, and to give his life a ransom for many' (Mark 10:45).

This is the long-range goal that draws Jesus forward, guiding the overall shape of his ministry decisions. As the unique Son of God, this calling has been predetermined for him before the foundation of the world. Its relevance for us, in this context, lies in our becoming aware that he chooses to pursue an overall purpose in his life, one that will finally take him to the cross. While this long-range goal does not necessarily guide him in what to do in every moment-by-moment decision, it does provide him with a broad compass bearing. It also enables him to avoid succumbing to the wishes of others when they tried to seduce him into taking an alternative long-range goal.

Because his long-range goal is clear, for example, he is not enticed when the crowd wants to make him their king. Instead, he takes evasive action: 'When Jesus realised that they were about to come and take him by force to make him king, he withdrew again to the mountain by himself' (John 6:15). Again, because he is committed, under the guidelines of godly methodology, to the long-range priority of 'giving his life a ransom for many', he is equipped to reject Peter's demand that he give up the path of suffering and death.

> *Peter took him aside and began to rebuke him. 'Never, Lord!' he said. 'This shall never happen to you!' Jesus turned and said to Peter, 'Get behind me, Satan! You are a stumbling block to me; you do not have in mind the things of God, but the things of men.'* (Matthew 16:22–23, NIV)

Some commentators have conjectured that the eagerness of the Greeks to see Jesus, recorded in John 12:20–22, was associated with an invitation from them for Jesus to travel back to Greece with them in order to teach. Any such action by Jesus would have represented a significant change in his life's purpose. Whether this interpretation is valid or not, it is certain that Jesus 'answered' them (verse 23) with a statement reaffirming his priority to give his life in order to provide new life for others. He rejects any alternative central concern that would distract him and reaffirms his calling:

'Now my heart is troubled, and what shall I say? "Father, save me from this hour"? No, it was for this very reason I came to this hour. Father, glorify your Name!' Then a voice came from heaven, 'I have glorified it, and will glorify it again.'

(John 12:27–28, NIV)

Having prioritised his methodology and the central calling of his life, Jesus is equipped to avoid many of the potential side-tracks which could otherwise have cluttered and overloaded life.

To what extent is the clutter and overload of your life a reflection of the fact that you have not clearly enough defined the methods you can legitimately use, and the central purpose to which God calls you?

Jesus' Priority in Day-to-Day Decisions

But prioritising *how* we may do things, and what the central compass bearing of our life is, will not always make it clear what we should do in making day-to-day, or even moment-by-moment, decisions.

Jesus had his central purpose fixed, but how did he know on one occasion that it was all right to break into what he was already doing to instantly heal a woman with a haemorrhage (Mark 5:21–34), yet on another occasion to deliberately delay action for two whole days when Lazarus was critically ill (John 11:6)? How did he know what the day-to-day priorities of his life should be?

First, let us be clear that he *did* establish day-to-day priorities, and that these certainly saved him from overloading to some extent by minimising the fragmenting of his energies.

Second, he did not simply accede to the expectations of others. This is dealt with more fully elsewhere in this book, but for our purposes here, it is important to see that Jesus *chose* where he would put his energies from day to day. He set priorities even at the level of what he would do with each day. There is, of course, no surprise in this. Long-term goals are not reached without following an overall plan that requires prioritising at the daily level. Although he did not carry a diary, it is apparent that he did something in his day-to-day planning which was the equivalent of planning in a diary!

We see Jesus prioritising at this day-to-day level, for example, when we read in Mark 6:45, 'he dismissed the crowd'. If you think about that crowd, you will rapidly conclude that among this group of people there were undoubtedly those who would have been happy to stay on in the hope of seeing Jesus do more amazing miracles. There would have been elderly folk, nervous about starting back on the way home at this hour. There would have been children and young people, ready to stay up all night and enjoy the adventure of it all. There would have been young couples, happy to stay longer and watch the moon rise over the lake and the stars come out. But Jesus takes control. We see him making decisions about how his time now needs to be spent. He does not let the crowd have all the control. He says in effect, 'OK, folks, time for you to head home now. Off you go.' And they go. Then he proceeds to do the next thing on his day's agenda. We read, 'After saying farewell to them, he went up on the mountain to pray'.

Or notice the account Mark gives us of the raising of Jairus' daughter. We are told that, as Jesus heads off to Jairus' place, 'a large crowd followed him' (Mark 5:24). When he hears a little later that the girl has died, we see him taking control at a much tighter level. The account is quite clear: 'He allowed no one to follow him except Peter, James and John' (verse 37). How did he do this? We can't be sure, but it sounds like he probably turned to the crowd, along with his other disciples, and said something like: 'OK, now I know you all want to follow me and see what happens, but I need some space right now. Please stay here and don't follow. I won't be too long.' Somehow or other he took control.

Next we see him taking control at Jairus' house. We read in verse 40: 'They [the mourners] laughed at him. *Then he put them all outside*, and took the child's father and mother and those who were with him, and went in where the child was' (emphasis added). Jesus does not allow the curiosity of the crowd, or the scepticism of the mourners, to dictate to him at this time. He has a different focus, and it is this priority that motivates his specific actions in this situation. He puts the mourners out.

Or consider Mark 9:30–31:

> *They went on from there and passed through Galilee. He did not want anyone to know it, for he was teaching his disciples.*

Once again, we clearly see Jesus following his priority for this period of time – instructing his disciples. He takes action to guard himself from interruption so that he can do what he needs to do. He sets, and follows, day-to-day priorities that arise from his overall life-call. It is as though he has checked his diary and discovered that, for today, the agenda is disciple-teaching.

It is obvious that in Galilee, where he and his disciples were travelling at that time, there were sick people needing healing, downtrodden people needing someone to stand with them against oppression, hungry people needing provisions, lost peo-

Thinking through your priorities will bring a sense of control to your life.

ple needing spiritual direction, and idolatrous people needing to be torn from their idols. But at this moment, in this place, Jesus is focused on another priority. He actively seeks to avoid these other tasks so that he can attend to the immediate priority.

Now this is reassuring. It is not just a picture of Jesus actively setting today's agenda. It is also a picture of him actively avoiding, and shielding himself from, other demands. It is OK to take the phone off the hook, to turn off the answering machine, to book family time and recreational time into the diary so we can more easily say, 'Sorry, I've already got something on that night'. It is OK to actively ward off other demands in order to give ourselves to each day's priority.

How noticeably this approach contrasts with much of what we try to do in day-to-day living! I (Cliff) freely admit that often my major struggle in the area of overload seems to be with excessive fragmentation. How can I balance the competing demands of a professional psychology practice, keeping up with professional reading, being a husband and father, being an elder in my local church, preparing lectures and workshops, writing, lecturing, contributing to leadership in organisations, doing maintenance work around the house, and so on? Chances are, if you are reading a book on overload, it is because this is your struggle too.

What can we do? We see Jesus prioritising, but we wonder *how* he determined his day-to-day priorities, especially when several were in competition.

It seems clear that for Jesus these daily priorities arose out of his ongoing communication with his Father.

> *'I am able to do nothing from Myself – independently, of My own accord, but as I am taught by God and as I get his orders. [I decide as I am bidden to decide. As the voice comes to Me, so I give a decision.] Even as I hear, I judge and My judgment is right (just, righteous), because I do not seek or consult My own will – I have no desire to do what is pleasing to Myself, My own aim, My own purpose – but only the will and the pleasure of the Father Who sent Me.'* (John 5:30 AMPLIFIED)

Now we could turn this into simply another burden – another big guilt trip. 'Oh, no. Here we go again. Now I've got to get up while it's still dark and pray for hours, just to get my daily instructions.' Whoa! Relax! This is not another demand. It is simply a recognition that this was part of the secret for Jesus in getting his daily road-map clear. It was not the whole secret. Some of his daily guidance came out of having his long-range priorities worked out, and refinements came as he asked his Father what *his* 'will and pleasure' was for this day, this moment.

The truth is that this need not be an exhausting, time-consuming activity. God already knows the sincerity of our hearts. If we really mean it, we need only ask him: 'Father, this is what I've got on the books today. But please change any of it, or exercise mid-way corrections along the way, according to what you want for me. I want your priority to direct my life today.' He'll take us at our word.

Another thing that may be helpful is to include in our prayer a specific request for God to protect us from people who will consume our time to no useful purpose, or from phone calls that will distract us (again to no useful purpose) from the priorities of the day. Not infrequently, as I (Cliff) have prayed this prayer, I have found someone cancels a counselling session, or there is a period when the phone is strangely quiet. It's kind of nice! He *is* actively involved in my daily life. Somehow the load seems more manageable.

Flexibility within Priorities

And yet, it is important to keep some flexibility in our prioritising. Just as it is clear that Jesus set priorities and sought to follow them, so that he would not simply let the world tell him who he was, it is also clear that he kept some flexibility in his daily life.

We have already seen, for example, that he allowed himself to be diverted briefly in order to heal a woman with a haemorrhage, at a time when he was already on a critical mission of mercy (Mark 5). On another occasion, after choosing to leave the crowd in order to have a break, the people hurried around the lake ahead of the boat that Jesus was in. By the time the disciples and Jesus arrived in the boat the crowd was there again. Moved with compassion for them, Jesus chose to put aside his agenda in order to spend more time teaching them – and, on this occasion, even feeding them.

We need to leave room for the compassion that is of God, which on occasions will cause us to revise our short-term priorities.

However, even with this flexibility, he set boundaries. When it was needed, as we have already noted, he dismissed the crowd and went off on his own to spend time with his Father being renewed (Mark 6:31–46).

We need to prioritise. It will help us to ward off some of the fragmentation that will otherwise threaten to overload us. But we also need to maintain some flexibility so that we do not become immovably legalistic. We need to leave room for the compassion that is of God, which on occasions will cause us to revise our short-term agenda.

Notes

1. The concept of mineral, vegetable, animal and human 'kingdoms', along with other aspects of this chapter, including some of the questions at the end, originated in The Walk to Emmaus renewal weekend, a program derived from the Cursillo Movement. The Walk to Emmaus is a program sponsored by The Upper Room, part of the Board of Discipleship of the United Methodist Church in the USA.
2. I first heard this example quoted by a speaker at a Suicide Prevention day programme run by Youth For Christ. Efforts to find the original source have, so far, been unsuccessful.
3. D.C. Glass and J.E. Singer, *Urban Stress: Experiments on Noise and Social Stressors*. New York: Academic Press, 1972.

 **SUMMARY**

■ Much of the overload that we experience comes out of the fact that we fail to clarify our priorities in life.

■ We see in the life of Jesus a model of one who set priorities, both in life-goals and methodology.

■ Because these life-goals were in place, he was able to handle the competing expectations, demands and pressures brought upon him in his daily life.

■ Much of our overload undoubtedly comes from the fact that we have not adequately clarified our priorities in methodology and life-goals. To do this prioritising provides us with a scalpel which trims away much of the excess with which we otherwise will contend.

■ Even when such prioritising has been done we need to retain some flexibility.

Your personal Overload Check-up

1. How much thought have you given to the selection of your methodology in business, relationships, church life, and so on? Do you use methods to achieve your purposes and goals which are not godly? If so, what changes do you need to make?

_____

_____

_____

2. List the medium and long-range goals you see as important for your life.

_____

_____

_____

_____

_____

3. To test the extent to which you are actually living with a focus on these goals, try answering these questions honestly:

- What do I spend my time doing?

  _____

- What do I spend my money on?

  _____

- What do I 'treasure' in my heart?

  _____

- What do I think about?

_____

_____

- What do I enjoy talking about? ('Out of the overflow of the heart, the mouth speaks', Matthew 12:34, NIV.)

_____

4. Compare the things you believe are your life priorities (Question 2 above) with how you actually live (Question 3). Are there obvious disparities? Are you living your life for things that you do not really see as consciously chosen priorities? What changes do you need to make?

_____

_____

_____

_____

_____

_____

Chapter Two
Setting Limits

Foundations

One of the greatest difficulties many of us face as Christians is in the area of setting limits. Somehow we have taken on board the mistaken notion that God wants us to flog ourselves along, doing every bit of good that comes our way, meeting every need that crosses our paths. We have made a virtue out of *not* setting limits; we have made a virtue out of the incredible folly of always saying yes to people's requests.

Perhaps part of the problem is that we have been carried away by the idealism of pioneer missionary William Carey's statement that he would rather burn out for Jesus than rust out! The words sound so saintly and noble, and most of the time we are reluctant even to examine such deeply-held convictions. But we need to. Without in any way diminishing the greatness of Carey's contribution to the Kingdom of God, we need to ask: Is his life a model we should follow, or was he, to some extent at least, a man driven by his own personality? We are certainly not equipped to judge, but we need to know that he went to India against his first wife's wishes. She was already emotionally unstable, and later in India she went quite psychotic before her death there. It is difficult to sort out what was of God and what was part of this great man's personality, but not particularly of God.

Who among us has not been impressed by the radical commitment of missionary C.T. Studd, who gave up a family fortune, as well as fame as an international cricketer, to serve God as a missionary in India, China and Africa in the early part of this century? Surely that kind of radical, 'no-limits' Christianity is what we should strive to emulate! But is it? In our assessment of C.T. Studd's life, have we been honest enough to acknowledge that others could not go at his pace, and that his incredible demands broke the health and hearts of some other missionaries? Do we recognise that his standards produced such a crisis in WEC's missionary work in Africa that he would have been pulled off the field if he had not died?

The last thing we want to do in this book is to disparage in any way the monumental contribution of Christians such as Carey and C.T. Studd. But it is time to appraise their contributions more honestly. We do not want to follow them where God is not leading us.

Or maybe we have been impressed by the saying 'The devil never sleeps', and we have thought that we had better not take any break or set limits either. If our opponent is on the job all the time, how can we afford to loaf? Now, even if that saying is true, at the very least we had better not rush to take Satan as our model! We had better check out what *God* asks of us – what his strategy is for his children.

When we stop for a moment to consider God as our model, we quickly realise that he did rest – on the seventh day. And he asked his people to give a priority to resting one day in seven.

So perhaps the first question we need to ask, drawing on the life of Jesus, is this: Was Jesus a workaholic? Was he driven to do, do, do? Is he the model that has produced this incredible disease of raising clouds of dust for God?

Was Jesus a Workaholic?

The answer to this question is important.

No one had a more demanding task than Jesus when he came to earth. His task was to share the good news of his Father's Kingdom and call people to repent and receive that Kingdom (Mark 1:14–15). Along the way he would be required to teach people about his Father and the Kingdom. There was a lot of correcting of misinformation to be done – the Pharisees and religious leaders had done a good job of circulating legalism and elitism among the Jews. There were acts of compassion to be undertaken – healing, raising the dead, providing for people's physical needs. And, of course, the goal was for the message to be spread throughout the whole world, without the aid of TV cameras, radio, the print media or the web. We would not be surprised if, faced with a task of this magnitude, Jesus just never stopped.

But is that what we find? Did Jesus show himself to be a Type A personality, unable to stop because of the importance and size of the task entrusted to him?

The answer is an unequivocal no!

Now this is not to say that Jesus did not push himself to the limits of his physical endurance at times. Of course he did. When he slept in the boat in the middle of a storm, we can only assume he was pretty much exhausted. He had given out to meet people's needs to the point where he just had nothing left to give. Sure, he pushed himself to the limit at times during his ministry.

God made us to be human beings not human doings.

But that is not the same as saying he *always* pushed himself to the limit, or that he was a workaholic. It is apparent from Scripture that Jesus *did* set limits.

Perhaps the clearest statement of this is Luke 5:15–16:

Yet the news about him spread all the more, so that crowds of people came to hear him and to be healed of their sicknesses. But Jesus often withdrew to lonely places and prayed. (NIV)

Do you get the force of that description? Jesus 'often' pulled out of the pressure and busy-ness in order to focus his life, spending time with his Father. This was the pattern for all the years of his ministry. Friends who study Greek tell us that, even though the word 'often' is not included in all translations of this verse, it is clearly implied in the Greek. This was his custom. It was his frequent pattern of action. It is not the behaviour of a workaholic.

There was almost no limit to the demands on Jesus, the needs surrounding him. On one occasion, recorded in Mark 3:20, a crowd was gathered at his family home in Nazareth, and so much was happening that Jesus and his disciples 'could not even eat'. This is not the only time this happened. In Mark 6:31, we again find Jesus and the disciples so involved in helping and teaching that they do not have time to eat.

How did Jesus handle this kind of situation? We get an answer in the latter passage. His response is to turn to his disciples and say, 'Come with me by yourselves to a quiet place and get some rest' (NIV). This is not the action of a person driven and out of control in his need to be active. He can and will give himself fully in ministry when he knows that this is what his Father wants of him. But he will not always simply yield to the demands of those around who need him, even when those needs seem quite legitimate. He sets limits and arranges to rest with his disciples.

Always saying 'Yes' to people is not a virtue but extreme folly.

And he does not carry neurotic guilt about it!

Any 'big picture' study of the recorded ministry of Jesus will rapidly make it clear that he deliberately, and often, used the geography of the country to provide himself with retreat opportunities. He went out on lakes where it was hard for crowds to follow; he crossed to desert regions; he went up onto mountains to get alone; he walked with his disciples on journeys that took days to complete and involved camping out by the roadside. These are not the ways of a person driven by hyper-activity or compulsive about trying to meet everyone's need.

He will not always simply yield to the demands of those around who need him.

Although scholars are unclear about the actual duration of Jesus' ministry, most agree that it is somewhere between two and three years in length. It is not a long ministry. Yet even in this brief time, we have the record of Jesus withdrawing for a significant period away to the north, to the vicinity of Tyre and Sidon, deliberately wanting not to be known (Mark 7:24). While this is undoubtedly a period of reassessment of his ministry, it is also clearly a time of retreat. We would not be terribly wrong if we called it a kind of holiday. Workaholics do not take such breaks. They do not set limits.

But this stirs up another question.

Did Jesus Ever Say No?

How many times have you heard it said that Jesus never turned down a cry for help? While ultimately that may be true of people who made specific requests for help, it is not actually that simple. Clearly there were times when Jesus walked away from need, at least from generic human need. And there were times when he said, 'Wait. Not now.'

One of the most dramatic of these incidents is recorded in Matthew 8:18, a verse that we would normally simply pass over:

'When Jesus saw great crowds around him, he gave orders [to his disciples] to go over to the other side of the lake.' Think about that statement for a moment. The crowd with all its needs is pressing in on him, and Jesus virtually says to his disciples, 'Hey, guys, let's get out of here!'

Do we imagine that he had by now dealt with all the needs of all the people in the crowd? Or was there perhaps, still, a crippled man who had been helped to get there by his brother, hoping for a miracle of healing from Jesus? Was there that day a woman with a sick and dying child who needed Jesus' touch? Or perhaps some deaf folk, some blind, some with deformities, some with tumours that would take their life if left untreated? The record is that Jesus said to his disciples, 'Let's get away from the crowd'. There's no record here that he healed everyone (though we do have that recorded at other times). There's no indication that he met every need. Rather, the indication is that he and the disciples were worn out. They needed to get away. So they left. He did not always say yes!

Or consider the events in Mark's first chapter. Here we have a record that is perhaps the best depiction of 'a day in the life of Jesus'. From verse 21 we find Jesus teaching in the synagogue on the Sabbath, then healing a man with a withered hand. After that he goes to Peter's home, where he heals Peter's mother-in-law. They share a meal, then that night, after dusk has signalled the end of the Sabbath, they hold a healing service. Mark says, 'And the whole city was gathered around the door' (verse 33). Jesus heals 'many' who were sick and casts out 'many' evil spirits. But the text seems quite clear that he does not heal everyone, and the events of the next day confirm that there are still those who need healing. In terms of the need for human healing, Jesus has not yet completed the job here.

Next morning he is up early, 'while it was still dark', and goes out to a quiet place for prayer. While he is there his disciples find him and tell him that the people are back for more (verse 37). Presumably there is still more healing to do.

However, this time Jesus says no to that human need. He has

heard his Father's direction and it leads elsewhere. He says, 'Let us go on to the neighbouring towns, so that I may proclaim the message there also; for that is what I came out to do' (verse 38).

Numbers of commentators have written about the description in John 5 where Jesus heals the man by the pool of Bethzatha in Jerusalem. It is apparent that this was some kind of hospital setting, with many sick people gathered in the one place, not because there was any medical attention, but because from time to time a miracle of healing happened there for those who bathed in the water (verse 4). On this occasion, a Sabbath, there are 'many invalids' there, including people who are 'blind, lame and paralysed' (verse 3). Yet Jesus only heals one person. Because he has done this healing on the Sabbath, the inevitable criticism comes from the Pharisees, but that is not the main focus of our interest here. On this occasion Jesus tells why he has done what he has done, and this answer presumably also explains why he has not done other things – such as healing everyone who was there. Jesus says: 'Very truly, I tell you, the Son can do nothing on his own, but only what he sees the Father doing; for whatever the Father does, the Son does likewise' (verse 19).

Jesus did not always say Yes!

Are we taking Jesus' words too literally if we presume that, as he walked among the sick people that day, he 'saw' in some way (perhaps through a momentary vision or some other form of revelation) that his Father wanted to heal this man? And so he does what he sees his Father doing. This, presumably, also explains why he does not heal everyone else. He had no inner confirmation that this is what his Father wanted to do on that day.

Here Jesus is operating out of an intimacy of relationship with his Father that is very deep. Although we so often lack this depth of intimacy, it is a vital resource for us in helping us distinguish between legitimate human needs (which unfortunately are limitless and can rapidly overload us), and what God wants us to do. And so, on this day, in this setting, in the mystery of God's sovereignty, one man receives healing and other needy folk are passed by. Jesus has not attended to their physical needs, even though these needs are obvious.

One more example. In Acts 3 we have the record of the healing of the crippled man at the temple. Peter and John are going up to the temple in the afternoon to pray when this beggar calls out for alms. Peter, inspired by the Holy Spirit, heals the man. The man is over forty years of age (4:22), and it is his regular practice to be placed at the entrance to the gate of the temple ('daily', 3:2). We know that he is a well-known figure because, after his healing, the people recognise him 'as the one who used to sit and ask for alms at the Beautiful Gate of the temple' (3:10). Are we going too far to suggest that, given these conditions, Jesus must surely have passed by this man on occasions when he went to the temple? It certainly seems most likely. Yet if so, apparently he never addressed the man's obvious need for healing. It was left to Peter and John, on a later occasion, when they perceived that this was what God wanted to do, to be the instruments of healing through the Holy Spirit.

Jesus did not try to meet every need he saw.

Clearly Jesus is compassionate (Matthew 9:36), but compassion does not always, or only, determine what he does, or when he says yes to the needs of those around him. For Jesus, central weight is given to the question: 'What does my Father want to do here? That's what I want to be obedient to.' Perhaps too often, in our need to meet others' needs, we say yes to what the Father is not calling us to. And so we pay a price, breaking down under the overload. There is truth in the statement 'God will not bless what he does not initiate!' It is important for us to know that, while compassion is an important value in Jesus' life, it is not the *supreme* value.

Look at that statement again before you go on. It is centrally important in our understanding of Jesus and in our following of him. Many people live as though compassion *is* the supreme value. The big picture of Jesus' life, however, indicates that, for him, moment-by-moment obedience to his Father, and commitment to Truth, have pre-eminence.

The cumulative evidence suggests that Jesus does not try to meet every need he sees. And, at least on occasions, this omission is tantamount to a no to obvious situations of need.

Sometimes Jesus Says 'Wait'

At other times, while Jesus does not say no, he does not rush to heal either. It is as though he says, 'Wait'. This, too, may be an interesting contrast to the way we try to go about things.

Consider, for example, the story of the Canaanite woman. She wants him to heal her daughter, but Jesus does not want to be identified as a healer in this situation. He wants to get away from human need for the time being. Matthew's description almost makes Jesus appear rude: 'But he did not answer her at all' (Matthew 15:23). Apparently his ignoring is not just momentary, because finally the disciples cannot stand the situation: 'And his disciples came to him and urged him, saying, "Send her away, for she keeps shouting after us".'

Eventually Jesus talks with her, and, after noting her unusual faith, does heal her daughter. But it is not an immediate response, and there is certainly some ambiguity about what has been going on here. Most of the sermons preached about this story over the years have maintained that he was simply testing her faith, but somehow that hardly seems to do justice to the text. The impression from Matthew seems to be that he did not initially intend to heal at all.

Matthew records another unusual healing in the story of the two blind men (Matthew 9:27–31). The blind men follow Jesus as he is walking along, calling out for his attention. The record says that they cried out, 'Have mercy on us, Son of David!', but it is clear that they are seeking restoration of their sight. The interesting thing is that Jesus apparently does nothing to meet their request while they are walking along the road calling out. He heals them later on when he has entered a house (verse 28).

We can reasonably infer that he does not want to draw more attention to himself (and bigger crowds), and that perhaps this is why he carries out the healing in a more discreet way (not surprisingly, the two men cannot keep the secret and his fame continues to spread). Be that as it may, once again we are faced with a story where Jesus clearly does not yield to the pressure of the moment to heal on the spot. He appears a lot less rushed in his response to this situation, and a lot more deliberate, than we often are.

But enough. If our contention here stands, then Jesus did not always meet every need around him. Instead, he recognised that it was important to remove himself from people at times, even if this meant leaving behind unmet human need. He set limits.

What Does This Mean for Me?

If we are struggling with issues of overload in our lives, we have to set limits. We have to learn how to say no.

This should never be an excuse for becoming lazy, or uninvolved in ministry, or self-indulgent. We are exhorted by Jesus to be like him (John 13:12–17), and he clearly gave priority in his life to doing what the Father called him to. Knowing that his ministry would only be a brief one, he recognised a kind of urgency about it in his words in John 9:4: 'I must work the works of him who sent me while it is still day; night is coming when no one can work.'

But it is also apparent, from a close look at his life, that Jesus did set limits and did not try to do everything. We are not being untrue to him if we seek, prayerfully and wisely, to do the same. False guilt may arise sometimes because of our religious conditioning – our church which has led us to believe that 'real Christians are always busy for God'. Perhaps now is as good a time as any to begin freeing ourselves from that 'yoke of bondage' (Galatians 5:1) by testing every new demand (as well as old ones). Ask: Is God the one who calls me to this, or is it my own ego or the pressure of other people's demands?

It remains true that God will not call us to more than he will equip us to handle!

 ## SUMMARY

■ Some of our greatest 'models' of Christian service may have contained an element of striving that was not of God. We need, at least, to think through what they have modelled for us.

■ Jesus was not a workaholic. He often withdrew for prayer and renewal.

■ Jesus did not always try to meet every need. Clearly, on occasions, he walked away from human need.

■ Jesus did not always act immediately when people wanted him to. At times he seemed to say 'Wait'.

■ If Jesus truly serves as our model, then it is all right for us to set limits or boundaries in our functioning. Our primary task is to try to hear what God is calling us to. We simply need to ask him to clarify, each day, his calling for us.

Your personal Overload Check-up

1. What are the specific responsibilities and roles that I currently carry?

_____

_____

_____

2. What expectations do others have of me in these roles and responsibilities? Are these reasonable? How do I respond to the expectations of others?

_____

_____

_____

3. What expectations do I have of myself in these areas? Am I reasonable with myself, or do I operate from some false notion of 'I have to do everything that people ask of me'?

_____

_____

_____

_____

4. When did I last say no to a request from someone? Do I use this limit-setting capacity?

_____

_____

_____

5. Specifically, what are the three areas of responsibility that generate most 'overload' for me? (It is important to be as specific as you can here. Do not respond with 'my job' or 'my children'. Try to get it down to concrete aspects such as 'having to give negative feedback to employees on Tuesday mornings' or 'the failure of the kids to pick up their dirty dishes from the TV room'. Specifics can be adjusted or worked on. Vague generalities are too defeating.)

_____

_____

_____

6. Generate an Action Plan for changing one of these three areas and commit yourself to undertake the necessary work.

_____

_____

_____

_____

_____

_____

_____

_____

_____

Chapter Three

Sharing the Load

Foundations

Sometimes we get into trouble because we try to do things all on our own. You may be familiar with this letter, written by a bricklayer who had tried to repair hurricane damage on his own.[1]

Respected Sir,

When I got to the top of the building, I found that the hurricane had knocked some bricks off the top, so I rigged up a beam with a pulley at the top of the building and hoisted up a couple of barrels full of bricks. When I had fixed the building, there was a lot of bricks left over. I hoisted the barrel back up again and secured the line at the bottom, and then went up and filled the barrel with the extra bricks. Then I went to the bottom and cast off the line.

Unfortunately, the barrel of bricks was heavier than I was, and before I knew what was happening, the barrel started down, jerking me off the ground. I decided to hang on, and halfway up I met the barrel coming down, and received a severe blow on the shoulder. I continued to the top, banging my head against the beam and getting my fingers jammed in the pulley.

When the barrel hit the ground it burst at the bottom, allowing all the bricks to spill out. I was now heavier than the barrel, and so started down again at high speed. Halfway down, I met the barrel coming up, and received a severe injury to my shins. When I hit the ground, I landed on the bricks, getting several painful cuts from the sharp edges.

At this point I must have lost my presence of mind, because I let go of the line. The barrel then came down, giving me another heavy blow and putting me in hospital. I respectfully request sick leave.

Yours, etc.

*Often we get into trouble because we have
not learned to share the load!*

The Case of Moses

In some ways this was the kind of situation Moses found himself in.

> *Now the people complained about their hardships in the hearing of the Lord, and when he heard them his anger was aroused. Then fire from the Lord burned among them and consumed some of the outskirts of the camp. When the people cried out to Moses, he prayed to the Lord and the fire died down. So that place was called Taberah, because fire from the Lord had burned among them.*
>
> *The rabble with them began to crave other food, and again the Israelites started wailing and said, 'If only we had meat to eat! We remember the fish we ate in Egypt at no cost – also the cucumbers, melons, leeks, onions and garlic. But now we have lost our appetite; we never see anything but this manna!'*
>
> (Numbers 11:1-6 NIV)

Moses has experienced the incredible series of miracles carried out by God in order to free the Israelites from slavery in Egypt, culminating in the parting of the Red Sea. Now the Israelites are free – all two million or more of them![2] But suddenly the burden of being the leader of such a huge number of people, especially when they are caught up in complaints, is too much for Moses. He feels completely overwhelmed. It is just too much for one man to handle. He tells God.

> Moses heard the people of every family wailing, each at the entrance to his tent. The LORD became exceedingly angry, and Moses was troubled. He asked the LORD, 'Why have you brought this trouble on your servant? What have I done to displease you that you put the burden of all these people on me? Did I conceive all these people? Did I give them birth? Why do you tell me to carry them in my arms, as a nurse carries an infant, to the land you promised on oath to their forefathers? Where can I get meat for all these people? They keep wailing to me, 'Give us meat to eat!' I cannot carry all these people by myself; the burden is too heavy for me.' (Numbers 11:10–14, NIV)

So God instructs Moses to bring seventy elders together.

> The LORD said to Moses: 'Bring me seventy of Israel's elders who are known to you as leaders and officials among the people. Have them come to the Tent of Meeting, that they may stand there with you. I will come down and speak with you there, and I will take of the Spirit that is on you and put the Spirit on them. They will help you carry the burden of the people so that you will not have to carry it alone.' (Numbers 11:16–17, NIV)

These leaders and officials were to be given the same prophetic Spirit that Moses had so that they could help him share the load. They would help him 'carry the burden of the people' so that he did not have to carry it alone.

> So Moses went out and told the people what the LORD had said. He brought together seventy of their elders and had them stand around the Tent. Then the LORD came down in the cloud and spoke with him, and he took of the Spirit that was on him and put the Spirit on the seventy elders. (Numbers 11:24–25, NIV)

It seems apparent that Moses had a tendency to feel like he was the only one who could do things. Perhaps he tended to operate like a 'one-man band' at times! On this occasion, God calls him to choose men with the character to be leaders, and God takes the Spirit that Moses has and puts it on these others.

In our work for God, it is vital that we learn to look for others who have the potential (in terms of character and general respect from people) and to bring them before the Lord, asking him to take our anointing and place it on them also.

A similar account to that above is recorded on the occasion when Moses' father-in-law, Jethro, visited the Israelite camp.

Share the Responsibilities

The next day Moses took his seat to serve as judge for the people, and they stood around him from morning till evening. When his father-in-law saw all that Moses was doing for the people, he said, 'What is this you are doing for the people? Why do you alone sit as judge, while all these people stand around you from morning till evening?'

Moses answered him, 'Because the people come to me to seek God's will. Whenever they have a dispute, it is brought to me, and I decide between the parties and inform them of God's decrees and laws.'

Moses' father-in-law replied, 'What you are doing is not good. You and these people who come to you will only wear yourselves out. The work is too heavy for you; you cannot handle it alone.

Listen now to me and I will give you some advice, and may God be with you. You must be the people's representative before God and bring their disputes to him. Teach them the decrees and laws, and show them the way to live and the duties they are to perform. But select capable men from all the people – men who fear God, trustworthy men who hate dishonest gain – and appoint them as officials over thousands, hundreds, fifties and tens. Have them serve as judges for the people at all times, but have them bring every difficult case to you, the simple cases they can decide themselves. That will make your load lighter, because they will share it with you. If you do this and God so commands, you will be able to stand the strain, and all these people will go home satisfied.'

Moses listened to his father-in-law and did everything he said. He chose capable men from all Israel and made them leaders of the people, officials over thousands, hundreds, fifties and tens. They served as judges for the people at all times. The difficult cases they brought to Moses, but the simple ones they decided themselves.

Then Moses sent his father-in-law on his way, and Jethro returned to his own country. (Exodus 18:13–27, NIV)

Jethro's words have a ring of wisdom about them. He can see that Moses is trying to carry too much of the load, and his summation is fairly blunt: 'What you are doing is not good. You and these people who come to you will only wear yourselves out.' His advice is two-fold.

First, Moses should teach the people how God wants them to live, so they can do a fair amount of self-monitoring of their actions.

Second, Moses should select others to help him with the work. *They are to be selected on the basis of their character, not necessarily their skills.* They should fear God, be trustworthy and be strongly opposed to dishonesty.

The lesson is clear. If we want to live without being crushed by the load, we need to learn to share the responsibilities with others who are capable and whose character attests to their potential. It may be that we need to train them, and it will be important to set aside time for prayer, asking God to gift them with the same anointing that he has given to us.

This approach, carried out prayerfully, would save many of our leaders from the overload they feel and the subsequent burnout that usually follows.

Moses reminds the people how he came to the point of needing to take on other leaders.

Avoid Overload

At that time I said to you, 'You are too heavy a burden for me to carry alone. The LORD your God has increased your numbers so that today you are as many as the stars in the sky. May the LORD, the God of your fathers, increase you a thousand times and bless you as he has promised! But how can I bear your problems and your burdens and your disputes all by myself? Choose some wise, understanding and respected men from each of your tribes, and I will set them over you.'

You answered me, 'What you propose to do is good.'

So I took the leading men of your tribes, wise and respected men, and appointed them to have authority over you – as commanders of thousands, of hundreds, of fifties and of tens and as tribal officials. And I charged your judges at that time: Hear the disputes between your brothers and judge fairly, whether the case is between brother Israelites or between one of them and an alien. Do not show partiality in judging, hear both small and great alike. Do not be afraid of any man, for judgment belongs to God. Bring me any case too hard for you, and I will hear it. And at that time I told you everything you were to do. (Deuteronomy 1:9–18, NIV)

Whenever we get to thinking 'I have to do this whole thing on my own' we are in danger. Yet for many people this is one of the driving assumptions behind their feelings of being trapped and overloaded.

It may be, as it was with Moses, that there are some tasks we have to do. But almost always we can break the task down into sub-tasks, and we can seek other people with the character or potential to assist us by taking on some parts of the overall task. That way, tasks can be accomplished which otherwise would be excessively stressful for any single person to accomplish.

Nehemiah was another who did it that way.

The Case of Nehemiah

Nehemiah was moved by God to undertake the rebuilding of the protective wall around the city of Jerusalem in the years 445–425 BC.[3] The Jewish exiles had been allowed to return from Babylon, only to find that their beloved city was in ruins. The task of rebuilding the walls was a monumental one, not just because of the size of the job but because there were enemies around who actively worked against the project. The people's hearts were discouraged.

What did Nehemiah do? He simply broke the task down into bite-size chunks and assigned an area to each available family. Priests, servants, perfume-makers, goldsmiths, men and women from all the surrounding towns were encouraged by Nehemiah's example, and all worked together.

> *Eliashib the high priest and his fellow priests went to work and rebuilt the Sheep Gate. They dedicated it and set its doors in place, building as far as the Tower of the Hundred, which they dedicated, and as far as the Tower of Hananel...*
>
> *Uzziel son of Harhaiah, one of the goldsmiths, repaired the next section; and Hananiah, one of the perfume-makers, made repairs next to that. They restored Jerusalem as far as the Broad Wall...*
>
> *Shallum son of Hallohesh, ruler of a half-district of Jerusalem, repaired the next section with the help of his daughters...*
>
> (Nehemiah 3:1,8,12, NIV)

Sharing the load like this enabled this monumental task to be completed in just fifty-two days. As well as heading off burnout, learning to share the load enables miraculous things to be accomplished.

The Case of Elijah

Elijah was a great prophet, and a great servant of God, and he was mightily used by God. But like Moses, he struggled at times with the sense that everything depended on him.

After the big shoot out with the priests of Baal on Mount Carmel (1 Kings 18), he fully expects that his enemies will just quit. Unfortunately, Queen Jezebel is not about to admit defeat. She vows that she will have Elijah killed, just as he killed her priests. Depressed and fearful, Elijah walks for forty days out to Mount Horeb, the mount of God.

On the mountain, Elijah experiences earthquake, wind and fire, but discovers that this time God is actually in the gentle stillness, not in the spectacular events. God asks, 'What are you doing here, Elijah?', and Elijah answers: 'I have been very zealous for the LORD, the God of hosts; for the Israelites have forsaken your covenant, thrown down your altars, and killed your prophets with the sword. I alone am left, and they are seeking my life, to take it away' (1 Kings 19:9–10).

> *We are always in danger of overload when we fool ourselves into thinking that we are the only ones who can do it and that 'everything depends on me'.*

God recommissions Elijah, giving him a number of tasks to carry out. Then he tells Elijah: 'Yet I reserve seven thousand in Israel – all whose knees have not bowed down to Baal and all whose mouths have not kissed him' (NIV). It is actually a rebuke for Elijah. 'You aren't the only one. You don't need to live as though everything rests on you and I am powerless.'

Somehow on the solitary path that he has followed, Elijah has come to believe that everything depends on him. He has been living as though he is the Managing Director of the universe. He should have known that there were others still faithful to Yahweh, because he had met one loyal follower, Obadiah, just prior to the contest on Mount Carmel. But no, he carries the weight of 'I'm the only one left'. There's a fair bit of 'poor me' in Elijah at this point!

We are always in danger of overload when we fool ourselves into thinking that we are the only ones who can do it and that 'everything depends on me'. One-person bands overload!

What Stops Us Sharing the Load?

Many times when we are feeling overloaded, the problem may lie in the fact that we have tended to overrate our importance, seeing ourselves as the only ones who can do the job. At other times we are over-burdened because we view ourselves as the only ones who can do the job *well*! Others can do it, but they would not do it up to the standards that we like to set.

All these are simply ego-driven enticements to overload, even though we often try to justify them to ourselves. At our worst, we even affirm that we are sure God wants it this way.

Often, underneath this attitude of 'I have to do it all myself', we are simply acting out of unacknowledged pride. At other times we have simply not adequately learned the skills of asking for help. Or we have not learned to accept help from others. Sometimes we have simply not learned what Moses had to learn, the skill of delegating.

Each of these areas may well be a growth area for you if you are a person struggling with a sense of being overloaded.

 SUMMARY

■ We set ourselves up for overload when we operate like a 'one-person band'.

■ Scripture records the example of Moses as an overloaded leader who was led to share the load by delegating.

■ People set apart to carry part of the load should, among other things, be specifically prayed for, that the Holy Spirit will equip them for their tasks.

■ Nehemiah serves as another example of a leader who avoided overload – and who managed to accomplish mighty things for God – by breaking big tasks down and sharing the load with others.

■ Part of our sense of overload may well be the misguided belief 'I'm the only one who can do it'. We need to submit our ego to God and regularly resign from the position of Managing Director of the universe!

Notes
1. Copyright, The Gerard Hoffnung Partnership. Used with permission.
2. Figure taken from the *Ryrie Study Bible*, note attached to Exodus 12:37.
3. *Ryrie Study Bible* note.

Your personal Overload Check-up

1. To what extent do I see myself as a person with the tendency to try to do everything myself?

_____

_____

_____

2. What motivates me to try to do so much on my own? Distorted pride – believing that no one else can do it? A need to be seen as someone who works incredibly hard? A fear of things being out of _my_ control?

_____

_____

_____

_____

Something else? To what extent am I just meeting my own needs in the way I hold control to myself?

_____

_____

3. Can I identify specific areas of responsibility where I take excessive ownership? If so, what are they?

_____

_____

_____

4. What are the attitudes and skills that I would need to change or improve in order to increase my capacity to delegate wisely? Is there a person I can talk to for guidance here, or a book I can read or course I can take that will grow me in these capacities?

_____

_____

_____

_____

5. Take time to choose one area of responsibility, and give some detailed thought and prayer to how you might share the load in this area? With whom could you share it? How would you approach any such person(s)? Is there any training you would need to help them with in order for the sharing of the task to be done wisely?

_____

_____

_____

_____

_____

6. Seek God's help in putting your thoughts in Question 5 into action. Review how it goes and adjust your approach accordingly.

_____

_____

_____

_____

_____

Chapter Four

With a Little Help From My Friends

Foundations

As humans created by God in his likeness, we were made for relationship. We do not function at our best when we function alone. Genesis 2:18 records that, from the outset of creation, God noted that 'it is not good that the man should be alone'. When we are isolated, cut off from the emotional support that friends can provide, life's pressures seem much greater.

The old adage 'a problem shared is a problem halved' also has application to stresses in life. As we face normal life pressures – grief, illness, loss, ageing, work stress, and so on – if we lack the support of fellow travellers, we are in danger of overload.

Psychologist Erik Erikson, writing about the eight stages of a person's life, recognised that the development of relationships was important throughout. However, in his theory he saw early adulthood as the period when this need peaked. Somewhere between the ages of twenty and forty, we face the life task of learning to develop intimacy, special closeness in friendships, in a way we have never needed to before.

This, of course, is the period when people usually marry. It is also the period when, for those who are single, deep friendships are usually established. We commit ourselves to spending our life with another person, or we give ourselves in deep friendship, learning to share not just part of our life, but the very depths of our life with another, or with more than one other.

Not surprisingly, it is not an easy task, and frequently people discover that they are not very good at allowing themselves to get close to others. Marriages and friendships break up. Others maintain an appearance, but really give up on the task of attaining intimacy. Sometimes people are frightened by the cost of attaining a deep level of sharing with another person.

Many things can make the task of meeting our deep, universal need for friendship difficult. Perhaps the most common obstacle is the quality of our early life experiences. If we grew up, for example, in a grossly dysfunctional family, where violence and abuse were perpetrated on us, then we may have learned, as a requirement for survival, not to trust people too much or get too close to them. The task of growing in intimacy can then be extremely frightening for us. Unconscious forces working within us can create many ways to help us avoid the work of building deep friendship.

Or perhaps our family was not grossly dysfunctional. It was simply that our parents were people of an earlier generation who had learned to switch their tender emotions off, so that we saw little intimacy modelled in their marriage or friendships. We sort of knew that they loved us, but they rarely said the words, and perhaps rarely expressed their love in hugs or through physical touch. They did not seem to have close friends of their own, so we did not see any demonstration of the skills needed to build or maintain friendships. Such a background can set us up for difficulties in early adulthood, having a need for deep friendship but lacking the understanding and skills which might help us to meet our need.

Settling for Isolation

Not infrequently, because the task of developing friendships frightens us or is too hard, we settle for other goals. We become workaholics or put our energy into making money; we devote ourselves to physical fitness or become obsessed with a hobby or interest. In one way or another, every one of these amounts to the same thing – settling for isolation rather than friendship.

Men, in Western society, have been on this road in unusually thick numbers in recent times. Many of the skills of friendship-building, such as sharing your feelings, have largely been denied men because they are somehow considered 'unmasculine'. The sad fact is that most men do not know much about building friendships. Men are often isolated, trapped by a set of cultural guidelines that make friendship-building very difficult.

But women are not doing so well either. Along with relationship difficulties, loneliness in some form would be the most common complaint for women who seek counselling at our clinic. Not surprisingly, many of these people are single. But what may be surprising is the number of women who are married but still struggle with loneliness. It is obvious that marriage, in and of itself, does not guarantee intimacy. The two people need to know how to reach towards each other in order to incorporate friendship in their marriage.

When the balance is wrong, when there is an excess of isolation and loneliness over intimacy and deep friendship in our lives, we are in overload territory. With no one to share with, no one to laugh and cry with, no one to talk with about the things going on in our lives, we much more easily cross over the border into being physically and emotionally overloaded.

Jesus As Our Model

Jesus, our model of the one complete human, demonstrates for us not only the need for friendship with others, but also the successful pathway to meeting this need.

It is important to realise that Jesus, as a single person, chose to meet his intimacy needs through sharing himself deeply in friendship with others, allowing himself to receive strength and support from them. For many of us, the person to whom we are most likely to turn to meet our intimacy needs will be a husband or wife. Of course, being married does not automatically guarantee friendship. Some of the loneliest people in the world

We need each other to get it right.

are married! But in marriage or in singleness, we must have friendship.

A striking passage in the Gospel of Mark alerts us to the importance of friendship for Jesus. At the time of choosing his disciples, we read, 'He appointed twelve, whom he also named apostles, to be with him, and to be sent out to proclaim the message, and to have authority to cast out demons' (Mark 3:14–15).

We recognise that the task facing Jesus was immense. It was no less than the task of bringing his message of a loving God, whose Kingdom is a present reality, to the whole world. Over the next few years he would give himself in preaching the good news about his loving Father, he would heal people and cast out demons, and he would teach, culminating in laying his life down at the cross as the ultimate sacrifice of his love for us. He needed a team to help him fulfil this goal.

Of the three reasons Mark gives for the choosing of the twelve, the first is the most important for our purposes. Jesus called them 'to be with him'. Undoubtedly, an important part of this is that in being with him they would learn from him. They would see him do things, they would receive his instruction and, as an outcome, they would be equipped for their part in spreading the Kingdom.

But there's more to it. Look at it again. I believe that his calling of them 'to be with him' was not just to have their manpower, but also their friend-power! His call to them so that they could 'be with him' was a separate, distinct and primary purpose. He recognised the need for a network of emotional support for himself as he confronted the opposition and challenges ahead. There would be times when their human presence would make the emotional difference he needed.

The Disciples – Jesus' Network of Support

Although Jesus had chosen the twelve to be with him, it is clear that three were especially close – Peter, James and John. There are different levels of friendship. We cannot achieve the deepest levels of intimacy with all our friends.

With Peter, James and John, Jesus shares his heart. He takes them with him to the scene of his first recorded raising of a dead person (Mark 5:37). He shares the stunning moment of his transfiguration with them (Mark 9), and takes them with him as he begins 'to be distressed and agitated' in Gethsemane (Mark 14:33). They are inclined to be bent reeds, or flickering candles, in terms of their emotional support, and undoubtedly he includes them as part of their apprenticeship, so that they can observe and learn from him. But we are not doing injustice to the text if we recognise that even their unreliable physical presence was of some emotional help to Jesus. It just helps to have friends with you!

And they were not complete failures. On one occasion, when the crowds are leaving Jesus because of his hard teaching, he turns to the disciples and asks, 'Do you also wish to go away?' Peter gets it right, speaking on behalf of the twelve. His words rise from a deep commitment to friendship with Jesus: 'Lord, to whom can we go? You have the words of eternal life. We have come to believe and know that you are the Holy One of God' (John 6:68).

Later John records that as Jesus sets out to return to Jerusalem – clearly at this time a dangerous place for him because of the plotting of the religious leaders – another of the disciples, Thomas, says 'Let us also go, that we may die with him' (John 11:16). Real friendship, this! It includes a readiness to die with Jesus.

Paul's Friendships

When we look at the life of Paul and contemplate the load that he undertook, venturing into foreign territory time after time, risking his life, enduring imprison- ment, torture, shipwreck, beatings, and so on, we are not surprised to see that he gave a high priority to the need for supportive friends.

On his first missionary journey he went in partnership with Barnabas. When they had a difference of opinion over the value of taking John Mark with them on their second missionary journey, Paul left Barnabas and teamed up with Silas.

Friends can bring encouragement and support which will release you to achieve much.

In many of his letters he writes of the impor- tance of the support of those around him. They were his fellow workers, but more than that, they were his friends.

Living on the edge of overload as he did, Paul found that the presence of these friends often made the difference between sur- viving and going under. They brought encouragement, joy and refreshment to his spirit. Because of their support, he was able to continue and to achieve much, even under the most testing circumstances.

Time after time, in our clinic we see the difference that friendships make to someone who is struggling.

Supportive Friends

I am happy because Stephanas and Fortunatus and Achaicus have come [to me], for they have made up for your absence. For they gave me respite from labour and rested me and refreshed my spirit... (Romans 16:17–18, AMPLIFIED)

But I hope and trust in the Lord Jesus soon to send Timothy to you, so that I may also be encouraged and cheered by learning news of you...Timothy's tested worth you know, how as a son with his father he has toiled with me zealously [serving and helping to advance] the good news. (Philippians 2:19,22, AMPLIFIED)

Tychicus...a much-loved brother and faithful ministering assistant and fellow servant... (Colossians 4:7, AMPLIFIED)

Onesimus, [our] faithful and beloved brother...
(Colossians 4:9, AMPLIFIED)

Luke the beloved physician... (Colossians 4:14, amplified)

[Timothy,] I yearn to see you so that I may be filled with joy
(2 Timothy 1:4, AMPLIFIED)

Get Mark and bring him with you, for he is very helpful to me for the ministry. (2 Timothy 4:11, AMPLIFIED)

Greetings to you from Epaphras my fellow prisoner here in [the cause of] Christ Jesus, the Messiah, and from Mark, Aristarchus, Demas and Luke, my fellow workers. (Philemon 23–24, AMPLIFIED)

Recently, a young wife, overwhelmed with the discovery of her husband's infidelity, drew strength to continue on from two special friends, a husband and wife, who gave her their time and their caring love. Without their friendship she may well have plunged into deep depression. Because of their support she is working through the grief of her broken marriage, not without pain, but with the firm conviction that she will make it.

A young man, suffering quite severe injuries as the result of a car accident and thus unable to travel by public transport, was recently brought faithfully to appointments by a roster of supportive friends, many of them driving more than an hour each way. Their friendship enabled him to get the help he needed, and now he is employed again and moving on in his life.

We need friends. We do not go well without them!

But what about when our friends let us down?

When Friends Fail

The story of Job chronicles the incredible loss and suffering of this man. Having lost all his children and all his possessions, and suffering a painful, disfiguring skin disease, he needs the support and encouragement of his friends. We read in Job 2:1: 'Now when Job's three friends heard of all these troubles that had come upon him, each of them set out from his home... to go and console and comfort him.'

So far, so good.

However, as Job pours out his woes, he finds that Eliphaz, Zophar and Bildad turn out to be no support at all. Rather than letting him pour out his anguish and just listening with care, they fairly quickly get into analysing the situation and advising him. All of them are convinced that, since he is suffering so much, he must have done some major wrong.

Job protests. He needs their caring support, not their condemnation.

> *To him who is about to faint and despair, kindness is due from his friend. Now to me you are like a dried-up brook... You see my dismay and terror and, believing me to be a victim of God's anger, you are afraid to sympathise with me.* (Job 6:14,21, AMPLIFIED)

Job's friends let him down when he needed them. In a way that should not surprise us. Friends are, after all, only human, and sometimes the thing that draws us together is not their sensitivity, but their directness. Friends can, and will, fail us at times. Job's friends certainly did. Jesus' friends certainly did. And inevitably, our friends will also fail us at times, just as we in turn will not be perfect for them.

From this awareness, probably the most important adjustment to make is to not expect friends to be perfect – to recognise that any close relationship increases the chances of being hurt at times. Of course, if the friend is hurtful all the time we would do well to seek friendship elsewhere. The overall balance is what is important.

Do not give up on friendships even if they sometimes hurt.

If you have been hurt by a close friend, consider the balance sheet. If the overall balance is considerably in favour of their support, encouragement, refreshment and love for you as you look over the period of the friendship, then they have truly been a friend. Do not give up on the friendship, even if there is a current hurt. It may be most important that you seek to heal it and grow the friendship even through the hurt.

We like to think that is what Job did. At the end of the book of Job we are told that, at God's direction, Job prayed for his friends. The implication is that they were forgiven by Job.

SUMMARY

■ As human beings, created in the likeness of God, we need friendship, we need relationship. We do not go well when we live in isolation. Genuine friends provide the emotional support that enables us to handle the pressures which may otherwise overload us.

■ Whenever there is an imbalance in our lives, with isolation and loneliness greater than intimacy and friendship, we are in overload territory.

■ At the outset of his ministry, Jesus appointed twelve 'to be with him'. He needed human support as he faced the huge tasks ahead of him.

■ Paul constantly gives testimony to the importance of supportive relationships in his life and ministry.

■ We can easily have unrealistic expectations of friends. Friendship is, after all, a close relationship between two imperfect people. We need to incorporate an awareness that friends may at times let us down, just as we at times may let our friends down. This is not a reason to give up on friendship, but rather an opportunity to work through to a deeper relationship. Friendship is vital; it is not an optional extra!

ACTION

Guidelines for Finding Potential Friends[1]

Since whole books have been written on the topic of friendship-building, it is unrealistic to aim to provide more than an introduction to the topic here. However, if this is an underdeveloped area for you, begin now to take action on it!

Research suggests that most of the potential friends that exist will share similarities with us in some way. Psychologist Steve Duck has written:

> Friendships are usually formed with people of the same religion and same socio-economic level, who have a similar job, similar background, similar educational history, similar level of income, similar recreational interests, and similar racial origins.[2]

This is important, because it gives us some guide as to where our best potential pool of friends lies. While it is possible for friendships to form between people who are markedly different, most friendships are made between people with some commonalities.

On the other hand, we need also to recognise that this does not mean we should look only for people who are completely same as us. Some of the attractiveness that we find in friendships often comes out of the *differences* that we bring to a relationship. He, for example, is more stable and reliable, while she is more spontaneous and fun. But usually, underneath these enriching differences there will be a considerable number of similarities.

Men generally find friendships develop around *doing* things with the other person – fishing, working together on a project, building, computing, playing sport, and so on. Frequently they do not disclose themselves at a very personal level, even though they see themselves as friends. Women tend to talk more over tea or coffee, sharing around common interest topics, and frequently revealing themselves more deeply than men.

It's easier to make friends with others who share your interests!

Obviously, too, the nature of friendships changes across the life-span. We usually spend more time together as friends when we are in adolescence or early adulthood. In later life, close friends may actually need only limited contact.

So if you are in the position of recognising that you need to invest some energy in developing friendships, then consider your capacities and interests and ask yourself how you might meet others who would share similarities. How might you find out about the capacities and interests of others where you work, at your church or within your community? And how might you reach out to them?

Getting Started

There are a number of important principles and skills that you need to be aware of in order to build friendships.

Become friends with yourself. Until you have come to a reasonable acceptance of yourself, warts and all, you will find it difficult to make use of the basic friendship-building skills. The person who lives constantly under the belief that they are useless, hopeless or unlovable is living from a position of having almost nothing to offer in friendship.

Accepting yourself does not mean thinking you are wonderful, nor does it mean fooling yourself that you do not have any cracks in your functioning! It implies a recognition that, for all your faults, you are still a person of value, because God created you in his image and Jesus has redeemed you.

If you have really not yet begun the journey of self-acceptance, it is time to take action. Seek counselling, get serious about reading and learning. Put into action what you learn, even if it feels difficult or different. It is the first step towards building deep friendships with others.

Work at improving your conversation skills. Conversing with others is a learnable skill, just like walking, talking, playing tennis, driving a car or operating a CD player. The first thing is to understand what the elements of a conversation are, and the second thing is to practise until you are comfortable with the skills.

The basic structure of a conversation goes something like this:

- A greeting is exchanged. (For example, 'Hello Tracy'.)
- Someone asks a question. (For example, 'What did you do on the weekend?')
- An answer is given. (For example, 'Let's see. Oh, on Saturday I went horse-riding with a couple of others from our London office. We try to go riding every month or so. It was really a nice day. Then yesterday, I visited our next door neighbour and her new baby at the hospital. Did a bit of gardening, too. Nothing much else.')

    The important thing here is to listen for any 'free information'. Free information is information that the other person discloses which they do not really have to. In the example above, the 'free information' includes: Tracy goes horse-riding regularly; her firm has an office in London; her next door neighbour has a new baby; she has a garden and works in it.

The good thing about free information is that you can safely ask more questions about any of it. It provides you with topics to ask about, or to note so that you can pick any of them up when there is a lull in the conversation. Obviously, when a person does not give any free information in their answer to questions, this makes conversing much harder – perhaps impossible!

- Two or three other questions are asked. These may be new questions or follow-up questions built on free information. Then there is a natural reversal of roles, with the other person asking questions. (For example, 'Anyhow, what did you do on the weekend? See any new movies?')

  Obviously the important thing now is for *you* to provide some 'free information' in response to the other person's question. You have to make a deliberate effort to provide some worthwhile content in your answers so it is easier for the other person to have topics to work with. Usually the best answers will be a paragraph or two in length. One word answers give the person nothing to work with, but page or chapter answers provide too much information!

- The conversation flows back and forth with each person taking turns asking questions and answering, listening and self-disclosing. Most new topics arise out of previously-given free information.

- The conversation is terminated by one person, or mutually. Usually this follows a convention, such as looking at your watch and saying something like, 'Hey, look at the time! I need to get going, but it's been really enjoyable catching up. We must do it again soon.' This type of termination contains reassurance for the other person.

When the format of a conversation is understood in this way, it makes the relevant skills quite obvious. They consist of *listening well* and *self-disclosing* at a reasonable level.

If you are unsure of your conversational skills, then the task is to begin practising. Take initiatives in greeting people and starting a conversation. As you practise you will get more comfortable.

Put yourself in the pool! If you are to build friendships, you need to mix with people. You will never improve your skills, or build your confidence, by hiding in the corner or avoiding social situations. If anything, behaviours like this will simply confirm your inaccurate, self-effacing conclusions such as 'I'm hopeless. No one could ever like me'. We have to take initiatives in order to meet and mix with others.

Maintaining Friendships

There are a number of qualities important for maintaining friendships.

Honesty. We cannot expect friendships to grow if we cannot be open with the other person. This does not mean being rude or insensitive. Some people think that being honest means you can tell the other person all their faults. That's covering our own rudeness with the label of 'honesty'. Honesty has more to do with being able to communicate without hidden agendas so that we are transparent – what you see is what you get!

We have to take initiatives in order to meet and mix with others.

Flexibility. Maintaining a friendship involves us in recognising that, over time, aspects of the friendship are likely to change. Our friend may marry, or have a child, or move, or develop other friendships. If we cannot accept these normal changes, and accept that they will inevitably affect the way our friendship works, we will simply become petulant and close down any friendship that changes.

We have to be able to accept the other person's additional relationships without jealousy. Real friendship is not ownership; it is a sharing of lives within limits.

Empathy. Genuine friendships require of us the capacity to put ourselves in the other person's shoes, to feel for them and to be able to communicate this level of caring to them. If we have this, we will be supportive when our support is needed and we will provide practical help when it is appropriate without being asked.

Notes
1. Much of the material in this section builds on ideas outlined in Peter Levin's book *Being Friends*. Collins Fount Paperbacks, 1987.
2. S. Duck, *Friends for Life*. Harvester, 1983.

Your personal Overload Check-up

1. How many close friends do you have? To what extent do they provide emotional support for you in times of overload?

_____

_____

_____

_____

_____

2. Using a scale of 1 (lowest) to 10 (highest), rate each of your friendships, first in terms of the equality of power, then in terms of the mutuality of interests.

_____

_____

_____

_____

_____

_____

_____

3. What have you done to develop friendships? How successful has this been for you? Do you need to begin again, working at beginning friendships?

_____

_____

_____

4. What do you do to maintain your friendships? Has this worked for you? Do you need to re-evaluate your approach?

_____

_____

_____

_____

_____

5. What has blocked you in the process of building friendships? How could you work to overcome these blockages?

_____

_____

_____

_____

_____

6. What capacities and interests do you have that could become connection points for developing friendships with others?

_____

_____

_____

_____

_____

_____

Chapter Five

Exercise and Diet

Foundations

A disclaimer to begin with. Neither of us is qualified to write anything specific on the area of exercise and diet. For specific information on exercise programmes and/or diets, we recommend you consult other people or books.

However, we have a few general things to say and we simply could not omit this external area completely from our book. If all sorts of other external changes and adjustments are made but exercise and diet are ignored, it may well be that the feeling of overload will simply continue.

Exercise

Most books on managing stress recognise the importance of some *regular* form of exercise. Usually advice is given suggesting that a person needs to exercise at least three times a week in order to get some physical benefit.

However, if the thought of three times a week sounds too much, do not be deterred from looking at other exercise options. We have come to believe that exercising even once a week brings an *emotional* benefit. Somehow the act of including some exercise in our weekly schedule serves to reduce our sense of overload.

The physical exertion certainly burns up excess adrenaline, the main chemical in the blood stream associated with feelings of being overloaded. That is why, after some form of physical activity, a tense, stressed person often feels a lot more relaxed, more mellowed. Adrenaline has been burned up. We also know

now that exercise stimulates the production of other chemicals, endorphins and enkephalins, in the brain, and these serve to provide natural feelings of well-being.

Not infrequently, overloaded people have quite harsh, punitive consciences that do not easily allow them to 'enjoy' exercise when there is so much work to be done. For married people, sometimes the guilt is also associated with the thought: 'It's not fair for me to play tennis/swim/play squash/whatever, when my spouse doesn't get an equal break!'

Recognising that this is a real issue, we suggest that, if you are married, you problem-solve so that each of you gets some kind of break, preferably one that involves exercise. The need for some form of re-creative exercise or activity exists for everyone, so some attempt to meet each person's need is important. Having done that, argue against any residual, false guilt. Remind yourself: 'I am giving a gift to my spouse/family/workplace by exercising. By doing this I am ensuring that I will be a better spouse/parent/worker.'

Important Guidelines

There are some important issues to be aware of if you are going to include some regular exercise in your week.

Choose an activity you find enjoyable. If you hate tennis, don't play tennis. If you hate jogging, don't jog. If golf stresses you more than it relaxes you, forget golf. If aerobics classes bore you, look elsewhere.

Often people make the mistake of taking up an activity that has no pleasure for them. As a result, they significantly reduce the likelihood of continuing in the activity. You are more likely to continue doing something that you find pleasurable, so make sure that whatever you take up is at least mildly enjoyable.

Exercise in our weekly schedule reduces our sense of overload.

You don't have to always beat your previous best time!

Find someone who will join you in your chosen exercise programme. If you are just starting, often it is difficult to maintain enthusiasm, especially when the going gets a little tough for some reason. The huge benefit that comes from having someone else involved with you in your exercise is that you help to motivate one another. When the enthusiasm of one of you wanes for some reason, the other person provides the emotional energy that helps you to keep going. You tend to encourage and motivate each other, and this helps build the programme into your schedule in a more stable way.

Some years ago I (Cliff) decided to swim at the local beach right through the winter. Now, I know that technically this fails Point 1 above, but I do have a mild masochistic streak which surfaces at times!

Swimming through winter might not present much difficulty for lots of people, but for me I knew it would be quite a challenge. Without a wet-suit (which, incidentally, only weaker mortals need!), I knew that I would face water temperatures around thirteen degrees Celcius at the coldest part of the season. My immediate tactic was to find someone to share the torture.

Brian is a good mate. Together we took the challenge – and, you'll be relieved to know, we made it!

What enabled us to keep going, heading down to the beach at 6.00 a.m. on windy, freezing mornings? The answer lies in the fact that, when everything inside me was saying, 'This is ridiculous', something else was saying, 'Get going. Brian will be here to pick you up any minute'. And so I dragged myself out of my warm bed. Of course, five minutes earlier Brian was checking over his sanity level, and fooling himself with the same sort of reasoning. While something inside him was saying, 'Get a brain. What are you doing?', another part of his mind was convincing him that I was eagerly waiting for him to arrive. And so he drove over. And so I joined him. And so we made it through the season.

The presence of someone else can make all the difference in establishing a regular exercise programme.

Guard against becoming too competitive. Overloaded people can easily make the mistake of becoming too competitive when they begin exercise programmes. This can easily turn the activity into overload.

You do *not* need to be the best! You do *not* need to win! You do *not* need to beat your previous best time!

If you have a competitive, Type A personality, then it is fine to play competitive sport. But it is not fine if it angers, frustrates and drains you. The exercise all of us *need* is enjoyable, pleasurable activity that burns up stress chemicals – not activity that produces more.

If you are beginning, build up gradually. Wisdom requires that no one go straight from an absence of exercise into strenuous activity. We recommend to people that they take a stress test and get a physical checkup before they begin. Having done that, follow a programme that involves a sensible build-up. There is no benefit for the overloaded person who ends up in hospital with a seized-up body!

The essential ingredient remains enjoyment. Find a way of making the activity enjoyable. If you jog, stop and smell the roses. Admire the gardens and trees while you walk. Share the activity with someone else and so multiply the pleasure. There is some enjoyable, re-creative activity for everyone. The task is to find it and build it into your weekly routine.

Virtual Diet

One client who appeared at a clinic where one of us worked was simply not handling the pressure. A twenty-seven-year-old engineer, he reported being completely overloaded at work. He put in long hours, pushing himself to complete projects by working through the weekend. Often he worked seven days a week.

Other areas of his life were not in balance either. Not surprisingly he was single, and he had virtually no friendships beyond a few work acquaintances. He simply did not have the time to develop supportive, mutually beneficial friendships.

His presenting problem was stress, but it centred around insomnia. He suffered from delayed sleep onset, often taking up to three hours to fall asleep. Even then his sleep was broken, and he was chronically tired.

Almost as an afterthought his diet was checked. He reported that he virtually lived on fast food and, incredibly, estimated that he was drinking up to twenty-five cups of coffee a day. To top it all off, he was a chain smoker.

While there were many underlying issues to be addressed, it was clear that his system was in a constant state of hyper-arousal because of the mega-doses of caffeine and nicotine it received. Whenever he laid his body on the bed and said to it, 'Time for sleep!', it was saying back to him, 'You must be joking! It's party time!' The beginning of help for him required some major adjustments to his food and drink intake.

Important Guidelines

This client illustrates the most important, simple guidelines relating to diet.

Be moderate in your intake of stimulants. Coffee, tea and chocolate are widely recognised stimulants. Some soft drinks also contain caffeine. While we do not advocate abstinence from these, we certainly advise that they be taken in moderation.

We suggest that overloaded clients should drink no more than four cups of tea or coffee per day. We suggest that they also control their intake of chocolate. Otherwise, the addition of caffeine to the body's already-excessive adrenaline is bound to contribute to the sense of overload and excessive tiredness.

Be aware that stimulants can help you feel better initially. This, of course, is the reason why people take stimulants when they are under pressure. A cigarette or a cup of coffee can 'settle the nerves'. Frequently when this happens, it is a sign that the body has begun to develop some dependency on the chemical.

However, even though there may be an initial feeling of benefit, there is always a longer-term price to pay. So do not be fooled into excessive intake of stimulants just because they initially seem to help. Somewhere, before too long, they will add to the overload on your system.

Be moderate in your intake of fast foods. One of the problems associated with overloaded people is that they rarely have time to prepare nutritious meals for themselves. Consequently, they often eat too much junk food.

The problem with an excessive intake of fast foods is that it leads to a diet containing too many unhelpful chemicals, including excessive fats and sugars. These in their own way add to the body's stresses. We recommend that fast food be eaten a maximum of once or twice a week, and that overloaded people aim to eat a healthy, balanced diet the rest of the time.

 **SUMMARY**

■ Any look at the external pressures operating on us which contribute to overload needs to address the issues of exercise and diet. For overloaded people, some attention to these areas is essential.

Your personal Overload Check-up

Exercise

1. Do I currently exercise regularly, or irregularly?

_____

_____

_____

_____

2. What exercise(s) could I undertake that would be enjoyable or pleasurable for me?

_____

_____

3. Would it add to the pleasantness of this exercise if I had someone to share the exercise with? If so, whom could I ask?

_____

4. In formulating my action plan
  • What will I begin with?

_____

  • How many times per week will I aim for to start with?

_____

  • When will I start?

_____

Diet

1. How often do I eat fast food each week?

_____

_____

2. How many cups of coffee/tea/cans of soft drink do I drink each day?

_____

3. What other stimulants am I aware of taking in?

_____

_____

4. What do I need to do to ensure that I begin eating a more healthy and balanced diet?

_____

_____

_____

Jogging and smelling the roses will be much healthier than eating junk food!

Part 2

Handling your internal world or

Learning to get over 'the Wall' more effectively!

Chapter Six

Redefining Yourself

Foundations

As we have already noticed, a great deal of our problem with overload is our own doing. We do the overloading, we maximise the perceived difficulties, and we accept much of the world's expectations, whether they are sensible and manageable or not.

We can achieve great gains in reducing overload when we find a comfortable balance among the many *external* demands. We feel less stressed when we reduce our number of evenings out, leave tomorrow's work at the office and begin to delegate the excesses in our lives. All of these are positive steps. The key is to keep it that way.

But a deeper problem lies in the fact that there are unconscious needs being met by having those things around. Believe it or not, we often allow ourselves to be overloaded because it meets some internal need. Unless we do something about *internal* reconstruction, there will always be a gradual regathering of those discarded and unstructured external stresses.

What we re-organise today, or even discard, we are in danger of picking up again tomorrow! So we are faced with uncovering and dealing with the internal reasons that allowed the external factors to get out of control in the first place.

Picture Michael Jordan stealing the basketball from an opponent and moving down court. He bounces the ball once, twice but on the third bounce – no bounce! The ball has stuck to the stadium floor. Boing, boing... plop! The ball has gone flat. The sphere is now a dome, flat on one end, curved on the other.

How come? Simple physics. Somehow the air pressure inside

the ball that is needed to keep the outside air from crushing in the 'skin' has been greatly reduced. The outside pressure is now too great, causing the 'skin' to cave in.

Whenever our inside pressure is less than the outside pressure, we too cave in. We call it 'burnout'. You cannot play good basketball with a flat ball, and you cannot live a full life with a deflated inner self.

What constitutes this inner self? There are a number of ingredients, including your *emotional maturity*, your *self-image* and your *spiritual maturity*. Let's look first at emotional maturity because it is a major player.

Emotional Maturity

Emotional maturity is a process, not a fixed position. We begin the process very early in life and continue until we are launched into eternity. It is not a matter of chronology, even though life experiences and biological and chemical factors may be contributors.

We begin the process when we learn to 'do for ourselves'. We begin to crawl, then walk, then climb. These are not just manifestations of our maturing physical system but also of our emotional growth. A child who is unaware of the world he or she is inhabiting, even if it is only the corner of a crib or play pen, is either too young, or has some deficit preventing him or her from being able to differentiate the outside world from self. Both of these are indications of restricted psychological and emotional development in the child.

The normal pattern of development sees the child increasingly exploring and expanding his or her territory. Psychologists call this a *separation and differentiation* process. Children gradually begin to differentiate self from the surrounding environment. By the time they are three or so, they can begin to endure some degree of isolation and have the beginnings of a measure of independence. When this normal process is blocked or delayed in some way, the child is more prone to be anxious and express a strong need for mother's presence.

Eventually most children can separate and become their own person. However, some of us make harder work of it than others. Whenever we are faced with a new task, we want 'Mum or Dad' in some form to be there to help us out, or we believe we must succeed on our own or we will be discarded, disgraced or disciplined. Either way, the adult who feels inadequate and seeks the approval of others, or the adult who feels inadequate and fears having to seek others in case approval is not forthcoming, are both struggling to some extent with the unfinished tasks of becoming an individual. Such a person has not yet progressed to an adequate degree in the area of emotional maturity.

The emotional maturity we seek is reflected in Luke 2: 41–52, where Jesus stays at the temple to talk with the religious leaders.

How we see ourselves dictates our actions and responses.

Here Jesus is twelve years old. While we might think this marks him as a child, in his culture he would have been seen as a young man. He was secure enough within himself to pursue what he knew was the correct course of action, even at the expense of disapproval from his parents. At the same time, he understood that he still had a need to connect to his parents, who would nurture his growth to where he would be able to stand alone.

When we can see ourselves as having the same choices as Jesus, we are maturing.

When we can see ourselves as having the same choices as Jesus, we are maturing. When, however, we feel compelled to stay connected to others in order to feel safe and avoid disapproval, this is a signal that we still have work to complete in order to fully separate and find our true self.

The emphasis is on choice. We choose to marry our spouses, we choose to develop our friendships, we choose to abide in Jesus. The maturing individual does not experience the pressure of *having* to connect and comply with the demands of others, because he or she sees self as separate and whole, apart from other individuals, the family, the company or the team.

Self-image

This leads us to a related factor – self-image. Self-image is the internal view we have of ourselves, the permanent picture we see inside that dictates most of our actions and responses.

Alfred Adler, a psychologist of the past whose work is still relevant today, believed that we act in every situation to protect our fragile self-image and overcome our deep sense of inadequacy. Adler may well be expressing in psychological terms what Scripture says about man as a created being, alienated from God, self and others.

If this is true, then the ball is always going to be a bit flat, and the external pressures greater than the internal.

The problem for many of us is that there is an incorrect view of the self. Basically it comes down to this. We are vulnerable to overload when, *in order to feel better about ourselves,* we take on inappropriate or irresponsible external loads. Everybody's self-image is vulnerable, and this makes it hard to say no to something that will enhance our internal image of ourselves. But when this leads us to overload, we simply trade one problem for another. We choose to give ourselves stress in the hope that it will combat our feelings of inferiority. It is not a good plan.

Chasing more simply creates more overload.

According to God's design we are the bearers of his image. We share in the personal life of God. We have dignity, worth and the capacity to know him because he loves us – *and nothing will alter this.* We may, because of life experience, feel angry at God or neglected by him. But Scripture assures us we are his special loved creation. Our Creator has shared himself with us. Genesis 1:27 gives us the account of this: 'So God created human beings, making them to be like himself. He created them male and female' (GNB).

This is really the only solid basis for a good self-image. Other options are poor. Public adulation, financial success, sexual conquests, material acquisitions, you name it – all give temporary satisfaction but have long term negative impacts on life. They never suffice, and chasing more simply creates more overload.

God's Kingdom – Or Mine?

A personal account is appropriate at this point:

In the late 1970s and early '80s I (Graham), like many Christians, was caught up in the post-Vietnam idealism and wanted to change the world. The thinking was something like this: 'If we can stop a war, we might be able to save the world for Jesus.' All by ourselves, you must notice. So I began to overload. (Actually good friends have told me since that I have always had the inclination to stretch myself to the limit!)

At this point, to my already full-time position as a campus missionary I added a part-time pastorate, the chairmanship of a Christian school, the intern directorship of a national training programme and the directorship of our area programme. I started building a house. Other family issues were also pressurising me; one of my sisters became terminally ill, and my wife was expecting our third child.

In January of the next year I went overseas and spoke at approximately two dozen meetings over a period of one month, returned home and proceeded to collapse. The next weeks were occupied with stress tests, panic attacks and what I thought were heart attacks. This continued for six months.

Faced with unpleasant realities, I resigned from all but my campus ministry, and even that was reduced to a part-time capacity. But the real problem was internal. Even after I had offloaded the external stresses, resigning from all the positions I could and reducing my output to a minimum, I was still faced with the question: What drove me to overload? Why couldn't I say no to all of these opportunities?

I faced these questions over the next twelve months. At times I felt like Paul in Acts 9:30, when he was enjoying the public ministry he thought he was ready for and yet found himself banished home to Tarsus. The next verse says it all: 'Then the church throughout Judea, Galilee and Samaria enjoyed a time of peace. It was strengthened; and encouraged by the Holy Spirit, it grew in numbers, living in fear of the Lord' (NIV).

As I sat in my rocking chair I saw the church begin to flourish, the school stabilise, the organisation move ahead. All around me, the various things I had given up began to flourish. Just like Paul, I was sidelined; but God's work went on. What was to be my response?

I had to redefine myself. Who was I? Was I a child of God created in his image – gifted to do his Kingdom work? Or was I building my own kingdom instead of his? I realised that I had been unable to say no in case someone else said yes. I had not wanted anyone to think that I was shirking my important bit for God's Kingdom. Somehow, being involved in so many organisations and doing so many things was supposed to prove that I was a Christian leader, on the cutting edge of youth ministry. When I saw these inconsistencies in my self-image, I had to repent and rebuild my self-image on God's truth. I began planning to do one thing at a time and let others do what they needed to. With the help of God and the grace of close friends I was able to gradually do the necessary rebuilding, although twenty years later I know I still have to watch my overload tendencies.

Material acquisitions give temporary satisfaction and can have a long term negative impact on our lives.

Whenever we have unrealistic expectations of ourselves, such as 'I have to meet everyone else's needs', we lessen our ability to live in peace and harmony. And without that inner strength, we risk 'going flat' as a result of external overload.

We need to be honest with ourselves so that we do not promise what we cannot deliver. We all have a vital part to play in work and in Christian service. Not all tasks are equally glamorous, but Scripture does make it clear that all parts are necessary. Paul is making this point when he describes the Christian community as a body in 1 Corinthians 12.

The Spiritual Self

Define ourselves in Kingdom terms means that we define ourselves not in terms of *product* but of *process*. The issue of redefining ourselves in terms of our spiritual maturity fits right into this process.

> *Those who are spiritual discern all things, and they are themselves subject to no one else's scrutiny. 'For who has known the mind of the Lord so as to instruct him?' But we have the mind of Christ.* (1 Corinthians 2:15–16)

These verses remind us that the 'spiritual' person, the person controlled and maturing in the Spirit, has a grasp of reality not known by others. Included in that reality are two important truths:

- Pleasing other people and following *their* demands is not what God requires or expects of us ('they are themselves subject to no one else's scrutiny').

- The spiritual person has the mind of Christ to assist him or her in making judgments about life, including what they are called to do.

Paul expands on this concept of 'having the mind of Christ' in his letter to the church at Philippi.

If then there is any encouragement in Christ, any consolation from love, any sharing in the Spirit, any compassion and sympathy, make my joy complete: be of the same mind, having the same love, being in full accord and of one mind. Do nothing from selfish ambition or conceit, but in humility regard others as better than yourselves. Let each of you look not to your own interests, but to the interests of others. Let the same mind be in you that was in Christ Jesus, who, though he was in the form of God, did not regard equality with God as something to be exploited, but emptied himself, taking the form of a slave, being born in human likeness. And being found in human form, he humbled himself and became obedient to the point of death – even death on a cross. (Philippians 2:1–8)

This passage makes the point that the true self, as defined by God's Spirit, is Christ-like. It does nothing to simply meet selfish needs but has learned to say no when there is someone who can do it better. The true self, having 'the mind of Christ', sees others as more deserving than self. It gives dignity and worth to others and will not use others to further its own gains. The true self takes care of its own needs and the needs of others as though they were the same.

How does this relate to overload?

Having a correct view of self, including the spiritual self, permits us to set boundaries on our own abilities and allows us to promote others in their giftings and service. It does not allow us to use, or usurp, other people's positions, and in this we are protected from overload.

The bottom-line in Scripture says that all of us are special creations, made in God's image. We are flawed by sin, yet beyond this we are redeemed by Christ, and indwelt by the Holy Spirit in order to serve God. If we are going to successfully unload our overload, we must redefine ourselves in these terms. Our expectations must be real, our commitment to the process must be real, and our assessment of *our* contribution to both must be real.

 ## SUMMARY

■ If we attend to all the external changes necessary to reduce our overload, but fail to address the internal causes behind our tendency to overload, we leave ourselves vulnerable to falling back into the same position.

■ Giving ourselves to an ongoing process of emotional maturity so that we do not *have* to please people in order to feel good is a vital part of developing our inner life, and one that frees us from much of the inner pressure to overload ourselves.

■ Growing in our awareness of the reality that we are made in God's image, and that this does not depend upon our achievements for God, also frees us from the inner compulsion to keep proving ourselves by how much we do.

■ For Christians, the truest self is spiritual and is being conformed to the likeness of Jesus. Seeing ourselves in this light enables us set appropriate boundaries, as Jesus did.

Your personal Overload Check-up

1. How do I see the current 'balance' between my inner and outer self?

_____

_____

_____

2. To what extent do I still feel the need for the reassurance and approval of those around me? to what extent do I feel a real pressure to *have* to connect with others all the time? How far have I come in the process of individualisation?

_____

_____

3. What three descriptive words come to mind most readily as I think of who I am? If these are an indication of my self-image, how am I picturing myself?

_____

_____

_____

4. To what extent have I tied my self-image to pleasing others?

_____

_____

5. Do I need to give more effort to redefining myself in *biblical* terms? How does Scripture define me?

_____

_____

6. Do I expect *other people* to be pleased with my involvement in Christian service?

_____

_____

_____

7. Do I expect myself to be involved in helping with *every* task around the place?

_____

_____

_____

8. Do I expect other people to blame me if things go wrong?

_____

_____

_____

9. How happily can I affirm others in their involvement? How freely can I rejoice when others are given recognition?

_____

_____

_____

Chapter Seven

Learning to Relax

Foundations

The Bible does not seem to have much to say about the skill of relaxation, at least not directly. However, if we see the essence of relaxation as a matter of 'letting go', then perhaps the Bible is not so silent after all.

When we relax our grip on something, we let our grip loosen – we 'let go'. When we relax our muscles, we 'let go' of the accumulated tension and allow the muscles to come to some resting position. When we take a more relaxed perspective on an issue, we 'let go' of the stress-producing view that we had, in order to adopt another perspective that allows us to function without so much inner stress. Relaxation, at its core, is about learning to 'let go'.

The Bible does have some things to say about letting go. For example, we are encouraged, 'Cast all your anxiety on him, because he cares for you' (1 Peter 5:7). We could paraphrase this invitation from Peter this way: 'Let go of all your anxiety. Pass it over to Jesus.'

Now, we cannot simply do that. If we are anxious about something or someone, there is no non-anxious button at the back of our head that we can press! Is this invitation therefore worthless?

Of course not. We know that one thing that can change our capacity to feel emotion is a change of perspective on the situation. If I feel a situation is out of control, it may be perfectly natural to feel anxious about it. On the other hand, if my perspective changes so that I no longer feel the situation is out of control but is OK, I am unlikely to continue to feel the same level of anxiety about it. The situation has not changed, but my perspective has!

When Peter invites us to let go of the anxiety associated with a sense of overload, at the same time he gives us the key to help accomplish this. He reminds us to adjust our perspective so that we are functioning out of a greater sense of security, 'because he cares for you'. If we remind ourselves that the Creator of the universe, out of his love for us, watches over our life so that nothing can ultimately harm our glorious future with him, then we have a key that can help us to let go of anxiety. 'Who shall separate us from the love of Christ?' (Romans 8:35).

Another precious invitation from Scripture is the injunction 'Be still, and know that I am God! I am exalted among the nations, I am exalted in the earth' (Psalm 46:10). When we become still, we let go of movement, and we let go of noise. We would not do this verse an injustice if we translated it, 'Relax, and know that I am God'. Once again, we note that the writer does not simply give the instruction; he also gives us the truth that enables us to adjust our perspective so that we *can* 'be still'. He reminds us that God *is* exalted, God *does* reign!

Jesus extends a similar invitation in Matthew 11:28–30.

Relaxation is about learning to 'let go'.

> '*Come to me, all you that are weary and are carrying heavy burdens, and I will give you rest. Take my yoke upon you, and learn from me; for I am gentle and humble in heart, and you will find rest for your souls. For my yoke is easy and my burden is light.*' (Matthew 11:28-30)

These words invite us to let go of the sense of burden that we carry, because our Master is gentle and humble in nature, and he wants us to experience rest.

Much of the sense of overload that we carry comes out of the way we see things. We are sure that we are responsible. We are sure that terrible things will lie at our door if we fail in some way. We see with a perspective that puts all the pressure on ourselves. When we see things differently, the sense of being overwhelmed can shift.

One of the great examples in Scripture of changing perspective lies in the story of the Aramean (or Syrian) attack on Dothan in the days of Elisha (2 Kings 6:8–23). Elisha's servant wakes in the morning, goes outside and is terrified when he sees all the horses and chariots surrounding the city. However, Elisha sees differently, and he prays asking God to open the eyes of his servant. The servant's eyes are opened and he, too, suddenly sees everything differently. Behind the Aramean army's chariots and horses, he sees 'the mountain… full of horses and chariots of fire'. An angel army from God! From then on he does not carry so much anxiety. He sees things differently!

Now it needs to be said that Scripture does call us to be committed followers of Jesus. There is a cost side here. We are called to 'take up our cross daily' and follow Jesus (Luke 9:23). So there is a tension between 'taking up our cross' and 'taking his "easy yoke"' on ourselves. Somehow we are called to do both. We are to give ourselves wholeheartedly in service, but we are not to carry the sense that everything depends on us – because it doesn't!

We need to learn more of the secret that Paul is alluding to when he describes his method of functioning: 'For this I toil and struggle with all the energy that he powerfully inspires within me' (Colossians 1:29). There is 'toil' and 'struggle' for Paul, but he is being continually empowered by Jesus, who breathes energy into him!

In this chapter we want to focus for a while on ways of 'letting go', of relaxing, knowing that our purpose beyond the 'letting go' is to be energised continually by Jesus.

Research into Relaxation

Research has shown that, when we learn to relax the muscles of our body, we enable ourselves to begin letting go of the sense of stress that can so easily cripple us. By now there are literally hundreds of studies in psychological journals showing that relaxation methods are helpful to people who are experiencing stress and overload.

Relaxation training has been specifically shown to be beneficial for people overloaded with stress, people with chronic pain conditions, people who struggle with nausea (morning sickness or the after-effects of chemotherapy), people who battle insomnia, people with specific fears and phobias, people with certain kinds of blood pressure problems, women with Premenstrual Syndrome, and many other situations.

On the one hand, these studies could cause us to see relaxation training as some kind of panacea. That would be a pity. It is important not to overrate its significance. However, it is also important not to underrate it! We cannot ignore this research. Clearly, for people who feel overloaded, learning the skill of relaxing has some potential benefit.

The simple fact is that the skill of learning to relax is helpful for people who carry a sense of overload!

First, it is important to establish that relaxation is, simply, a skill. It is not magic, and it is not hypnosis. It is just a skill like learning to play the piano, hit a golf ball straight or land a tennis serve in the service court. As with all skills, you do not get better at it by reading books or by thinking about it. You get better by doing it!

Years ago, when I (Cliff) was learning the trumpet, I had a German trumpet teacher. He used to say, 'Cliff, from nussing come nussing'. At the time I was a little too young to figure out what he was really saying, so I tended to look wise and say 'nussing'. However, with the wisdom of the years I know now that he was really saying to me, in a gracious way, 'Cliff, you didn't do much practice this week'. If you do nothing, then you get nothing by way of improvement.

So it is with relaxation skills. If you practise, you will rapidly get better. If you do not practise, you will not improve. 'From nothing comes nothing!'

Stage 1 — Acquisition of the Skill

Many people have had some experience of Stage 1 – they have attended a stress management course, or listened to a training tape a number of times. That is good. However, it is important to be crystal clear on the purpose of this training. The purpose is simply to give you the skill so that you can access it when you need to. Stage 1 is about acquiring the skill.

There are many different ways of learning relaxation. Some exercises focus on going through muscle groups one at a time, letting go of tension. Other approaches focus on practising breathing slowly and deeply as a way of allowing your body to begin relaxing. Still other approaches use a guided meditation, or repeating self-instructions, to help you begin relaxing. Some approaches make use of positive and reassuring Scripture verses. The research shows that no one method is superior to others. The most important thing is to find an approach that feels comfortable for you.

The easiest way to accomplish Stage 1 is to get hold of a relaxation tape. There are plenty around. Inquire through your local hospital or through a psychologist.[1]

If you are unable to get hold of a tape any other way, the following is a sample script that you could get someone with a relaxing voice to put on tape. If you are a good reader, you could even put it on tape for yourself.

'I want you now to take a moment to get yourself comfortable. You may sit in a chair, feet comfortably and firmly on the floor in front of you, or you may want to lie on the carpet or on a bed. Just make sure that you feel as comfortable as possible. You may want to remove contact lenses or glasses, if you wear them. You may want to loosen a belt or tie, or make some other adjustment – just so long as you feel comfortable.

Relaxation is a skill. You have to make time for it.

'Now, close your eyes and take a moment to think about your breathing. Scripture records that in the beginning God breathed into humankind the breath of life. Your breath is a gift from God, given into your hands so that you might live. What a wonderful gift it is – taking air into your body and miraculously making use of that part of it, the oxygen, which your body needs, then expelling the rest. A natural, effortless process that goes on, whether you're waking or sleeping, thinking about it or not thinking about it. This is indeed a gift to praise God for! No wonder the Psalmist says, "Let everything that has breath praise God!" Take a moment to praise God for the gift of your breath. *(30 seconds of silence.)*

'Now, we're going to make use of your breath-gift to help your body relax. You will be in charge. Your breath has been given as a gift by God to you.

'I want you now to slow your breathing down just a little, and as you do, let your body relax and enjoy that feeling of relaxation, of letting all tension and stress go. Just slowing your breathing a little and relaxing as you do. Take a moment now to slow your breathing down and feel that pleasant feeling of relaxing. Go ahead now. *(30 seconds)*

'And as you breathe more slowly, I want you also to breathe that little bit more deeply, allowing yourself to relax even more. Breathe just a little bit more slowly and deeply, letting yourself relax and enjoying the feeling of using your breath-gift to be kind to your body. Continue to breathe more deeply and slowly. *(30 seconds)*

'And as you breathe more deeply and slowly, I want you now to make your breathing as smooth as possible. Make it such a smooth, gentle, unforced action that it almost feels as if your body does it without you. Such a smooth, even, relaxed action that all the jerkiness is gone – your chest just rises and falls smoothly as you breathe in and out. So smooth that it almost seems as though the change from breathing in to breathing out is unnoticeable, and the change from breathing out to breathing in is unnoticeable. Smooth and regular, slow and deep. It might help you to think of your breathing as being smooth like the long, flat arc of a swing, as it moves slowly and perfectly evenly back and forth to the rhythm of your breathing. Smooth as lamb's wool, or downy feathers. Very relaxing. *(30 seconds)*

'Keep on breathing smoothly and deeply and slowly. And

You get better by doing it!

now take a moment to review the various muscle groups of your body, making sure they are relaxed. Make sure that your toes and feet, your ankles, your calf muscles, your knees, your upper legs, right on up to your thighs and buttocks are relaxed, with all the tension gone. Make sure that your stomach muscles and your back muscles are relaxed. Just let all the tightness and tension go from them and enjoy the feeling of relaxation. Relax your fingers and hands, your lower arms, elbows and upper arms, right up into your shoulders. Relax your neck and scalp muscles; relax your face muscles – the muscles around your eyes and across your forehead; the muscles in your cheeks and around your mouth and chin. Allow your whole body to relax more and more and enjoy the feeling of being relaxed, safe and secure, warm and calm inside. *(30 seconds)*

'And while you continue to breathe deeply and slowly and smoothly, I want you to notice just how good your control over your body is. I want you to notice that in your hands there is the slightest increase in warmth, almost so slight that you may find it hard to notice, so slight that you may not even be able to detect it. But you may be just able to notice that slight increase in warmth. There is nothing magic about it at all. When you relax yourself, you open the blood passages up so that your blood can flow more easily and fully – and it tends to produce an increase in warmth in your fingers and hands. You're being kind to your body when you relax like this. You're making its work easier. Now continue to enjoy your control over your body for a moment longer as you continue to relax. *(30 seconds)*

'In just a moment I'm going to count back from ten to one, to give you the opportunity to re-orient yourself from your relaxed state. When I get to five, I want you to wiggle your fingers and toes just a little. When I get to one, open your eyes and re-orient yourself. You'll feel pleasantly relaxed, but fully alert, ready to go on with any task you have in front of you. OK? Ten... nine... eight... seven... six... five... wiggle your fingers and toes just a little... four... three... two... and one! Open your eyes and re-orient yourself. You may want to stretch a little. That's right. Allow yourself to gradually adjust to the external environment again.

'By practising this relaxation you will be able to learn to relax quite quickly, simply by controlling your breathing rate. You will be able to use this to shed feelings of being overloaded after a stressful time, or to reduce the sense of overload when you're going into a situation that you anticipate will be stressful. Remember, the key to success is practice. If you practise faithfully, at least once a day for several weeks, you will certainly be able to notice an improvement in your ability to feel less overloaded. You will feel calmer, more in control, more relaxed, simply by focusing on your breathing – making it slower, deeper and more smooth.'

Once you have a tape, or have put the above script on tape, you will need to practise. You do not have to kill yourself in this process. We recommend that you practise once a day for about ten or fifteen minutes. After about three weeks you will certainly find that your capacity to access your new skill of relaxation and to reduce your sense of overload will have improved dramatically.

Stage 2 — Application of the Skill

Stage 2 is incredibly important. Most people who have tried to learn to relax but found it of little benefit will discover it is simply because they failed to undertake this second stage. As we noted earlier, Stage 1 is about acquiring the skill. It is fairly useless if we are limited to it as if it was the complete package.

Learning to relax is similar to practising scales on the piano or hitting a bucket of golf balls at the driving range. Playing scales and arpeggios on the piano is not playing the piano. Playing the piano involves making use of the technique we have acquired by practising scales in order to play pieces of music. Hitting balls at the driving range is not the game of golf. But when we play the game of golf, we look to use the skills we have practised elsewhere. Just so, when we feel overloaded, we do not always have the option of saying to others, 'Hold on a moment. I just need to lie down here with these earphones on for twelve minutes. I'll be right back with you. Don't go away!' We need to be able to access the skill fairly instantly and weave it into the 'game' of unloading overload.

Here are some specific suggestions for putting your new 'de-overload' skill into practice.

Practise accessing the skill by simply taking one deep breath, and as you exhale, *let go* of the sense of overload.

Bring your level of stress down; allow yourself to feel more relaxed and in control.

Practise relaxing only parts of your body.

In other words, practise relaxing your stomach, arms and legs, as you sit talking with someone. They will have no knowledge that you are consciously accessing your relaxation skill.

Make use of the cue words 'Before', 'During' and 'After'.

To remind yourself to access your relaxation skill *before* you go into any stressful situation, *during* the situation or *after* the situation. Simply take a deep breath and allow yourself to feel more relaxed and in control. Sometimes, of course, you will not get any warning before you find yourself in the situation, so you will not be able to use the *before*; but use these where you can.

Look for frequently-occurring situations in your daily life, and use these to cue you into taking a deep breath and relaxing downwards.

One that we have found helpful is the ringing of the phone, which is often a stress cue for busy people. Train yourself to use this as a reminder to you to take a deep breath and relax, before you pick the phone up. Other useful cues can include stopping at a red light, going through a doorway, checking the time on your watch or a clock, entering a building or classroom, opening a filing cabinet, switching on a computer, completing a page of word-processing, getting a drink from the water cooler. Several of these are natural stress cues; so when you retrain yourself to use them to remind you to take a deep breath and relax, you are taking a significant step in reducing your sense of overload.

By making use of these applications of relaxation, you are in effect momentarily bringing your stress levels down at frequent points during each day. This means that you simply do not allow the sense of overload to continue to grow in the way it did before you acquired and applied relaxation (see diagram opposite).

Notes

1. The tape *Stress Management for Christians* by Cliff Powell and Graham Barker can be ordered from Christian Psychological Services, PO Box 640, Mona Vale, NSW, Australia 2103.

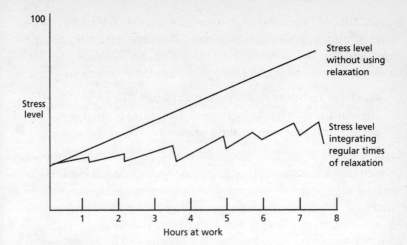

100

Stress level

Stress level without using relaxation

Stress level integrating regular times of relaxation

1   2   3   4   5   6   7   8

Hours at work

SUMMARY

■ While the Bible does not directly say anything about relaxation, it does encourage us, at a number of points, to learn to 'let go'. We are to let go of anxiety; we are to let go of activity and noise, in order to know that God is present; and we are to let go of the sense of carrying the whole yoke ourselves, and take on the yoke that is shared with Jesus – a yoke that is easy, involving a burden that is light. All of these injunctions have a relationship with the concept of relaxing and trusting in God's faithful presence in our lives.

■ There is a great deal of research to show that the skill of relaxation is an effective component in helping people function without the sense of being overloaded.

■ Learning to relax involves a two-stage programme. The first stage, Acquisition of the Skill, is usually accomplished by practising relaxing using a taped programme. The second stage, Application of the Skill, involves learning to practically access the skill during our normal daily activity, usually by using cues to remind ourselves to relax at regular points during the day.

Your personal Overload Check-up

1. What steps do I need to take so that I have a taped relaxation programme to practise with in order to acquire the skill?

_____

_____

2. When will I start practising so that I acquire the skill?

_____

3. What time of day would be best for me to make fifteen minutes to practise with the tape? Morning or evening? Some other time?

_____

4. What are a few frequently occurring events in my day that I can use as cues to remind me to take a deep breath and relax?

Event 1:

_____

Event 2:

_____

Event 3:

_____

Chapter Eight

Kingdom Living

Foundations

Have you ever wondered how Paul, the always-on-the-go missionary statesman, could ever write these words: 'Make it your ambition to lead a quiet life… so that your daily life may win the respect of outsiders' (1 Thessalonians 4:11–12, NIV)?

'Make it your ambition to lead a quiet life.' Could he write this because he was now in what Erik Erikson called the generative stage of life, that stage where we forget the bad in the past and attempt to pass on only the good? Or was it because he was now chained to a Roman guard and was ruing the problems he had encountered, feeling that maybe he had overdone things and was now paying for it? Or was he perhaps giving an encapsulated version of Jesus' Sermon on the Mount to an enthusiastic but overload-prone, infant congregation? Or was he just writing a do-as-I-say message, rather than a do-as-I-do one? How could he write 'make it your ambition to lead a quiet life'?

The quiet life. The contemplative life. What's it all about?

From the outset, we need to put aside all images of medieval monks, living their lives in isolation and deprivation in mountain retreats. That certainly is not what Paul, or any other biblical writer, suggests. Rather, the quiet life is a life guided by biblical priorities, examined values and focused purposes. In this chapter we want to suggest that it is intimately bound up with the development of the concept expressed in the Greek word *makarios*, which is usually translated 'blessed'.

Biblical Priorities

The priorities of life commanded by Jesus in his mountainside discourse include the basic ingredients for this spiritually inner-driven life.[1] Matthew records the Beatitudes in his fifth chapter.

First, these priorities encompass our relationship with the Creator-Father. Second, they speak to our relationship with other people. And lastly, they inform our relationship with our own self and circumstances. These areas of focus are not divided into neat sections in the passage but are woven throughout the discourse, suggesting that perhaps there is no real division between them, nor any stages or set patterns to follow. But certainly the 'Kingdom living' described in this passage represents a significant change from our usual results-driven lifestyle to more of a process experience, one where the inner life is nurtured along with the outer.

Most of us are wary of change, yet dream of major changes. We would love to leave the city for the simplicity of rural living, or we long to leave the uncertainty of country life for the dependability and predictability of the city. Dreams. Desert islands have their appeal, but only if they come with hot and cold running water. We dream, but we take action a lot less. The Beatitudes, however, call for active change in the way we live.

The inner changes described in the Beatitudes are changes that have ramifications for all areas of our lives. We recognise that they go against that part of our basic nature that we looked at in a previous chapter – that part of us that wants to prove our worth to others and to advance us at the expense of others. Yet having acknowledged this, these changes are central to learning to unload the overload.

Kingdom Life

When Jesus saw the crowds, he went up the mountain; and after he sat down, his disciples came to him. Then he began to speak, and taught them, saying:

'Blessed are the poor in spirit, for theirs is the kingdom of heaven.
'Blessed are those who mourn, for they will be comforted.
'Blessed are the meek, for they will inherit the earth.
'Blessed are those who hunger and thirst for righteousness, for they will be filled.
'Blessed are the merciful, for they will receive mercy.
'Blessed are the pure in heart, for they will see God.
'Blessed are the peacemakers, for they will be called children of God.
'Blessed are those who are persecuted for righteousness' sake, for theirs is the kingdom of heaven.
'Blessed are you when people revile you and persecute you and utter all kinds of evil against you falsely on my account. Rejoice and be glad, for your reward is great in heaven, for in the same way they persecuted the prophets who were before you.'

(Matthew 5:1–12)

Matthew begins by stating that Jesus sat down to deliver these principles. He is emphasising the point that this was a formal instruction period, one of high importance.

Jesus begins with the word 'blessed'. The Greek word is *makarios*, and it describes a joy that is serene and holds an internal secret which cannot be taken away by external circumstances. It carries a sense of unassailable wholeness. John, in his Gospel, quotes Jesus as saying that no one can take this *makarios* from us (John 16:22). It is always available and permanent. This stress-free *makarios* experience is connected to a number of principles.

Relationship with God

Makarios begins with our relationship with God. We are told that it belongs to the person who is poor in spirit (verse 3).

Depending on grace. The word translated 'poor' actually means 'destitute of everything'. The person who recognises that he or she is absolutely destitute of any personal resources, and who therefore clings to the grace of God, will have real inner, unshakeable serenity.

This is not an appeal for poverty but for priority. It echoes the book of Ecclesiastes, where the author tries out all of life's pleasures only to find that, in and of themselves, they are empty. Experienced as part of the process in the context of God's grace, they are good. But pursued as ultimate goals, they turn out to be husks.

So Kingdom living begins with a change from self-sufficiency to dependency on God's grace, recognising that apart from it we are impoverished.

Grieving over sin. In the second Beatitude, Jesus goes on to say that this *makarios* comes out of mourning. For many, the spiritual application of this has to do with 'grieving over our sinfulness'. It makes sense. We become Christians when we acknowledge our sin before God, when we are broken-hearted over Christ's death for us. Jesus is now saying that having an ongoing heart-felt awareness of our sinful nature keeps us close to him, and, in a secondary sense, keeps us from returning to self-adulation.

The usual response to deep mourning is to seek comfort and solace in human relationships, or in compensatory behaviours such as drinking, shopping or eating. However, in the context of our relationship with God, Jesus says mourning will receive comfort. It will bring an unassailable serenity to us. There is some indication that this mourning for sin creates a different inner response. Because of God's comfort, we can renounce our selfishness and relax in his forgiving grace at the same time.

So this Kingdom life begins with a change in how we structure our relationship with God. We need to live with the foundation of God's grace undergirding us. We recognise that ultimately we have no resources with which to cope. We are destitute and depend on him for everything we need. But this felt awareness of our sinfulness before God is joyously balanced by our acceptance of ongoing forgiveness. There is no need to stress over our past sins (or present ones for that matter). We live in a process of constantly mourning our sinfulness and simultaneously rejoicing in our forgiveness.

In real terms, this certainly translates into reordering our schedule to spend more time listening to, and learning from, God our Father, Jesus and the Holy Spirit. Developing the inwardly quiet life inevitably requires spending time in his presence.

One appealing aspect of the mystics of the past was their times of solitude and prayer. Do not expect that your spiritual foundation will be deepened on the run. I (Graham) have found Scriptures on tape a great blessing. In my schedule, it gives me sixty minutes in the car of absorbing God's word, three days a week. I do not see this as a substitute for regular times of meditation and reading but as a supplement to them.

How does your schedule look? If it does not permit such times, you are overloaded. Maybe more radical surgery on your commitments is needed. Could you move closer to your job? Could you change jobs to be closer to home? Could you go part-time, or change careers?

Whatever it takes will be worth it in order to begin the steps towards experiencing *makarios*. Our relationship with God is the key to Kingdom living.

Relationship with Ourselves

Jesus moves on next to deal with our internal relationship, our relationship with ourselves.

He notes that *makarios* belongs to the meek, who will inherit the world.

A balanced view of yourself. In our time, meekness is often thought of as passivity, spinelessness. To be meek is judged a weakness. It somehow suggests a person does not have the guts to stand up for his or her rights, and we all know how bad that is! In the Beatitudes, however, meekness does not carry these meanings, but rather a sense of the inner power of self-control. Aristotle identified it as the ability to attain a 'happy medium'.

The word translated 'meekness' was also used to describe domesticated animals. Significantly, at other times it was used as a word of contrast to the prideful arrogance of some nobles. It was also used to convey humility. Pulling all of this together, we could say that meekness is a kind of compound quality which includes moderation, self-control and self-awareness.

The writer of Proverbs reminds us that this meek quality is very powerful. 'One who is slow to anger is better than the mighty, and one whose temper is controlled than one who captures a city' (Proverbs 16:32).

Living a meek life as part of Kingdom living may mean swapping the ambition to hold a directorship for maintaining our dignity and integrity in the position we have. It may mean swapping our perceived rights to first place in a queue for the thankfulness that we are there at all.

Kingdom life is concerned with the avoidance of extremes, the control of impulses and the development of a balanced view of oneself. These are all internal qualities, developed by the person who has given some priority to growing meekness – the interior discipline that frees us from the 'have to's' and 'got to's' that so often drive us and overload us.

Hungering for righteousness. The next Beatitude that links in with our relationship with ourselves is the one that reminds us that *makarios* belongs to those who hunger and thirst after righteousness. We know what hunger and thirst are about, even if it is only via TV reports from drought-stricken countries, but we do not know much about righteousness. Most of our lives are lived in feeding our hunger and thirst for unrighteousness. Jesus is saying if we want the serenity and lasting peace of *makarios* we need to seek righteousness as if our life depended on it. There is a connection between joy in living and righteousness.

There are many books on this subject, but we want to suggest that the key to understanding this connection lies in the grammatical construction associated with the word 'righteousness' as it is used here.

Usually the verbs 'to hunger for' and 'to thirst for' are followed by what has been called the partial genitive case, indicat-

Developing the inwardly quiet life inevitably requires spending time in God's presence.

ing a desire for a part of the whole. For example, 'I'm hungry for some bread' means 'I want a part of the loaf'. If I wanted the whole loaf I would use the accusative case, a most unusual usage. In verse 6 Jesus uses the accusative case for 'righteousness', indicating that the hungering and thirsting is for the whole of righteousness, not just a portion. It seems that *makarios* belongs to those who have a constant and all-pervading hunger for righteousness, not just a part of righteousness.

A person may have external goodness and give philanthropically to charity but be unjust in dealings with employees. Or a mother may spend time reading to her children every evening but constantly remind them how fortunate they are to have such a caring parent. Both have a hunger for partial righteousness, or a form of righteousness, not a hunger for the whole of righteousness. *Makarios* people hunger and thirst after a righteous life in totality.

When we live with major inconsistencies between what we

say and do, what we do and think, or what we believe and act on, we set up conflict within ourselves and in our priorities and relationships. It is not that we do not want total righteousness. That would be nice. But we do not *hunger* and *thirst* after total righteousness because that would just mess up other things we want to do – the selfish things. So trying to satisfy both becomes a major stressor.

Jesus says focus on achieving the one and let him handle our other needs. He emphasises this when he asks us: 'But strive first for the kingdom of God and his righteousness, and all these things will be given to you as well' (Matthew 6:33). We need to offload the pressures we put on ourselves by simplifying our lives and wholeheartedly pursuing the just, the good and the healthy.

Relationship with Others

The third relational dimension in Kingdom living is our relationship with others.

Empathy and nurture. Jesus states that *makarios* is given to the merciful – that they themselves will receive mercy. This Beatitude strikes at the core of the two relational conflicts: our inability to be empathic with others, and our sense of rejection whenever others misunderstand us.

'Mercy' carries the sense of being able to enter into someone else's experience. It comes from the Hebrew word *chesedth*, which relates to the womb. Jesus is saying that those who connect or engage with people at an empathic level will enjoy a reciprocal relationship that produces great joy. The majority of people yearn for such intimacy but settle for casual contact, shallow sexual associations or serialised partnerships. Jesus is letting us know that to receive from others the quality of relationship we want, we need to give it first.

We will not have *makarios* if we simply use people and love things, rather than use things and love people. We will never find peace in isolation. Jesus says the need is to move past our defensive, detached lifestyles to enter into a shared relationship with others. Of course, it is not possible to do this with everyone at the same level. But it is possible to give to those with whom we live and work the dignity of time and empathic listening. We, in turn, will find the same from them when we need it.

What would it take to change our lives so that we incorporate this level of relationship with others? Basically it flows with, and out of, the earlier Beatitudes: living in humility, living with a mourning spirit, living meekly and seeking wholeheartedly after righteousness.

Consider the relief that could be experienced if our close relationships were nurturing. It would make other, more difficult relationships less stressful and problematic. If we live expecting to receive from others, we will always be disappointed; but if instead we live *giving* to others a 'womb experience' of deep emotional connectedness, we cannot be disappointed even if they do not respond. The reason is that we do not rely on a response from others to receive *makarios*. Jesus gives that to us himself.

Our inner world will become overloaded with negative attitudes if we are not experiencing God's presence.

When we consider living a life that is focused on relationship, we need to remember that each of us is prone to use our relationships for ourselves. All of us know that the larger stresses in our lives are usually other people. So Jesus says there is no advantage in living mercifully if your real motive is to use people to gain for yourself. This is what modern counsellors would identify as a characteristic of co-dependent people. Rather, *makarios* belongs to the person whose motives are genuine.

Pure in heart. This is where the next Beatitude comes in:

'Blessed are the pure in heart, for they will see God.' Here we are called upon to avoid mixed motives or pretense. We are to be WYSIWYG people – *what you see is what you get.*

The Greeks used the opposite of this word for 'pure' to describe alloy mixed in with a metal, or watered down drinks. A person whose relationships have ulterior motives cannot really enjoy the fullness of the relationship. The fear of discovery of loss will prevent such a thing. We need to be genuine – 'pure in heart'.

Making peace. Next Jesus says, 'Blessed are the peacemakers, for they will be called children of God'. Ironically, 'The Peacemaker' was the name given to an early American six-shooter made by Chris Colt, a gun that was particularly reliable and accurate. If you wore this gun and knew how to use it, you could put an end to an argument very rapidly. 'Peacemaker', then, was a name given to a weapon that could very swiftly bring about a solution to a problem. Those left behind, of course, quickly discovered that any such peace was very temporary!

Unconditional relationships encouarge purity of heart and bring peace.

To those who deal with troubles and situations in a peace-producing, Kingdom manner is given the title 'peacemaker'. Jesus was talking about our ability to be reconcilers, people who bring peace into situations. To be peacemakers we need to be able to ask ourselves: What can I do here to promote the glory of God and the dignity of this person? Sometimes this may mean confronting a problem, because to ignore it would mean it would inevitably accumulate over time. It may mean a call to struggle with realities we would rather not face.

Peacemakers seek resolutions, not the attribution of blame. Peacemakers do not focus on exacting revenge or retribution. The goal of peacemakers is to focus on the positives and work through the difficulties, drawing wisdom from the Spirit of God.

Out of this approach, our relationships with others take on a distinctly nurturing, rather than stressful, character. Peace*making* is more active than peacekeeping!

No compromise. Finally in our search for the elements of the contemplative life, we are confronted with the challenging statement that *makarios* belongs to those whose lives, because of their commitment to righteousness, evoke persecution. This is a challenge to a 'no-compromise' lifestyle.

The life that stands strongly for what is right, as Jesus did, will obviously be at odds with the wider world at various times. Problems, even persecution, will arise when our Christian walk means excluding unrighteous social practices, or when it leads to opposing tolerated but ungodly beliefs within society. Jesus did not advocate social rebellion. He began an inner revolution that promotes a love of others and a gentleness of spirit, while giving all the glory to the Father. However, he warns us that, while this gives great inner fulfilment, it is also likely to incite opponents to anger, and even aggressive persecution.

In developing this Kingdom life, one that can sustain us in the ongoing stresses and struggles, we have much to gain from learning and growing in the qualities Jesus commends in these Beatitudes. It is important for us to be aware that, even if we are growing in Kingdom living, we will still have to deal with those individuals whose stresses overload them and whose systems reward an aggressive lifestyle. A developed inner life will help immensely in managing the pressures inherent in relating with such people. Because this life, as outlined in the Beatitudes, centres on our ways of relating, it gives us a centre from which these parts of the external load can be better managed.

Notes
1. Still one of the best expository accounts of this Bible passage is *The Sermon on the Mount* by D. Martyn Lloyd-Jones.

# SUMMARY

■ Paul talks about the desirability of making a 'quiet life' one of our ambitions. While this sounds strange coming from someone who was so active in his Christian ministry, it is apparent that he is talking about our inner life, or what we call 'Kingdom living'.

■ The essential recipe for Kingdom living is outlined in the Beatitudes. The Greek word *makarios*, translated 'blessed', tells us the outcome of this kind of living Kingdom living, unlike overload living, brings an inner reward of 'blessedness' – an inner serene joy that cannot be taken from us.

■ The first element of Kingdom living builds from the establishment and maintenance of a right relationship with God. This needs to be nurtured in practical ways in our daily life. It begins with a recognition of our poverty of spirit before God, and a mourning over our spiritual condition.

■ The second element lies in the development of a right relationship with ourselves. Key ingredients at this point are the development of meekness and a hunger and thirst for righteousness.

■ The final element is the development of right relationships with others. Central to this is the development of a life active in mercy, purity of heart and peacemaking.

Your personal Overload Check-up

1. To what extent have I begun to seek the 'quiet life' that Paul urges us to seek after?

_____

2. Using a ten-point scale, where 1 = Extremely Distant and 10 = Wonderfully Close, how would I currently rate the closeness of my relationship with God?

_____

3. Does my relationship with God demonstrate a healthy 'poverty of spirit' and a mourning over my neediness before him? What would aid my growth in these areas?

_____

4. Which aspect of 'meekness', as it is described here, do I most need to grow in?

_____

5. How much do I hunger and thirst after the totality of righteousness? To what extent is my hungering and thirsting a _partial_ desiring?

_____

6. Would others see in me qualities of mercy, purity of heart and peacemaking? Which of these is God calling me to grow in at this time?

_____

7. If this quiet life as described in the Beatitudes, this Kingdom living, is available to me, what practical step can I take from this moment on to grow further in it?

_____

Chapter Nine

Renewing Your Inner World – 1

Foundations

We all 'construct' the world we live in, building it out of the people, events and experiences that we encounter in life. This constructing – or 'construing' as it is sometimes called – is not a conscious process. We do not usually sit down and figure out how we should think about people and the world. Our constructed version simply emerges out of the emotional, somatic and cognitive 'bits of meaning' that are activated in us by the people, events and experiences of our life.

This does not mean, of course, that there is no objective reality. It simply means that we, limited by our senses and receptors, cannot take in the total reality around us. We always end up living in our limited version of reality.

That would present us with problems enough, but even worse, we often convince ourselves that our little perspective on reality *is* Reality, rather than just our view of it. That certainly creates even more problems for us.

The point is made by thinking of a room full of people all looking at an object – say, a chair. *Everyone looking at the chair will agree that there is a chair, but the actual perspective on the chair that everyone has will be different.* No two people see it in exactly the same way. Everyone has a different slant on it, a different viewing angle. In fact, it is impossible for any two people to see the same 'chair'. The only way this could happen would be if one person could enter the other's body and look out through their eyes, and so get the angle that they have. And that is not possible either. Everyone agrees that there is a 'chair' in front of them, yet no two people actually see the same chair.

However, the example teaches us more. *No one person is capable of seeing all of the chair.* There are perspectives on the chair and dimensions of the chair that no one will ordinarily see. For example, there is a legitimate view of the chair to be found lying on your back underneath it and looking up at the seat, or jumping over it and looking down from overhead. These are real perspectives on the chair, though it would be unusual for anyone to view the chair from these particular angles. And then there are a countless number of angles. No single person can possibly see all these at any one time. I will always be limited by my particular angle on the chair, and I will never be able to see or take in the whole chair. I will always see little 'c' chair, never capital 'c' Chair.

So it is with all dimensions and areas of our lives. We always end up with a limited perspective or view on things. We never take in the whole. It is not possible. Our particular perspective on anything is shaped by the peculiar experiences we have been through in life, out of which we have 'constructed' our viewpoint or our world of understandings. For example, if I have been physically abused by my parents as a child, now in adulthood I will have constructed my own unique view on people ('don't get too close, they can be dangerous'), myself ('if my parents beat me, then I must be bad') and family ('it's a dangerous group of people').

Again, it is important to know that the construing I have done is not usually, or only, a process of thinking things through and reaching some conclusions. My world of meanings and understandings *is* my creation, but most of it has been constructed unconsciously. I did not consciously think about it. My body just took in information and began to react in certain ways at certain times. My emotions just responded in their own unique way to the people I encountered and the events and experiences I went through. And finally, as my capacity to think about things developed, my mind began to draw conclusions and develop its rules for living that now guide much of my behaviour. But the process is a holistic one, and I need to know that my thinking is not the only dimension that has constructed the reality I live in. Along with cognitive processes, my body memories, emotional responses and kinesthetic sensations have all contributed to the shaping of my world of meaning.

Now, it is very important to realise that much of the world of meaning that we create for ourselves, the reality that we live in, causes us problems. And in the world of overload this becomes particularly important. The distress of overload that I experience comes largely out of the world of meaning that I live in, the experiential reality that is my total way of viewing the world and handling the world. For example, if my parents were driven, Type A personalities who emphasised the importance of achievement and being productive, then very likely I will have taken this into my world of meaning also. Consequently, much of the overload that I experience will come directly from the way I view this part of life. I will tend to push myself harder and harder, and feel guilty if I cut back in order to relax.

The good news is that, if indeed I have created my own world of meaning (albeit much of it unconsciously), and if it is true that my world of meaning is *not* Reality (but only my constructed view of reality), then I can work to reconstrue my world of meaning in less stressful, more healthy ways. Of course, the question is how.

At this point, most psychologists or writers begin to stress the importance of renewing your inner cognitions or mind, and we recognise the importance of that. It is important to spend some time changing the way we think about things. But if the unique reality that each of us inhabits is constructed out of more than our cognitive knowings (our thinkings) – if it is constructed out of our emotional knowings (our feelings) and our somatic knowings (body sensations) as well; if it includes both conscious and unconscious knowings – then we also have to expose ourselves to new *experiencing*, not just new head knowledge. Only then will we change our world of meaning.

Renewing our inner world is more than renewing our 'mind'. Paul encourages us to 'be transformed by the renewing of your minds' (Romans 12:2), but it is important to see that he writes this in a context of advising us not to be 'conformed to this world'. He is concerned that our inner 'world', not just our thinking capacities (as suggested by the word 'mind'), should be different from the values and priorities of the external world that devalues God and the significance of our spiritual life. Perhaps a better translation of Paul's meaning would be 'be transformed by the renewing of your inner world'.

Because the inner world we live out of is made up of a lot more than cognitive material, we can see why many of the attempts to help people change by simply exposing them to new biblical truth are not sufficient. The new material may be included in the person's conscious, cognitive knowing, but other dimensions of the person's inner construing may be much more important in determining their functioning in the world. We have to find ways of taking cognitive truth and helping people to *experience* it, so that their inner world of meanings, cognitive and emotional, conscious and unconscious, is then adjusted.

It is important to spend time changing the way we think about things.

Paul did not just write about renewing the inner world. He practised it. In this chapter we focus on truths from his life that he wrote about. Some of these he specifically identified and encouraged others to put into practice. Other truths we simply deduce from his manner of writing and what we know of his life. But each of these guidelines is, in some way, a gem with great potential for helping anyone unload their particular overload. In particular, we draw from Paul's writings to the church at Philippi.

'Big Deal'

In Philippians, Paul is writing from prison in Rome. We know that he is under some kind of 'house arrest' – at times chained between two guards, at other times apparently able to receive visitors, and obviously able to dictate letters to the churches he has planted. So his situation is a kind of mixed bag. But, bottom-line, he is not a free man.

Even worse, he is facing a trial, or hearing, before the emperor. At that trial he will be questioned in order for the emperor to determine whether or not his Christian activities constitute a threat to the Roman empire. If the judgment goes the wrong way – and that could depend on the emperor's mood or digestive state as much as on the truth – Paul may well be facing the death penalty. He could be beheaded. (Oral tradition in fact tells us that this is eventually what did happen to Paul.)

Still more bad news. Apparently there are some power struggles going on among the Christian leaders in Rome. Now that Paul is out of the way, some are preaching 'from envy and rivalry' (Philippians 1:15), hoping to build up their particular following. There is a chance the infant church in Rome may be torn apart by internal strife. All in all, it does not look like Paul's situation is so great.

In the midst of this he writes: 'What does it matter? Just this, that Christ is proclaimed in every way, whether out of false motives or true; and in that I rejoice' (1:18). The first four words are important. 'What does it matter?' Other versions translate this, 'It does not matter'. In a way, Paul is surveying the external situation and coming up with a conclusion, 'It doesn't matter'. Not being Greek scholars we do not have access to the original language, but it would not be surprising if it was something like *bigos dealos*. Big deal! So what!

We need to see what Paul is doing here. He is putting a different perspective on his situation. He is viewing it through the lens of the truth that God is in control and his purposes are being worked out. In that light, why does Paul need to get his toga in a knot? He is adjusting his attitude to things so that they do not overwhelm him.

We have already seen that much of the stress and overload that we carry comes from the way we view things. If we can re-adjust our perspective from an overload-inducing one to a reassuring one, this will certainly help us.

As I (Cliff) write, today's newspaper contains an article about fences between adjoining properties, and the legal battles people have over them. Ms Wendy Faulkes, chairwoman of the Community Centre, notes, 'People have even had heart attacks'. The article reports the story of two neighbours who have had an ongoing dispute for more than fifty years over a tree planted by their fence (that's right, fifty years!). One neighbour reported, not surprisingly, that stress over the disagreement is aggravating her blood pressure problems – but she hopes she doesn't have to give in!

Another example: a small paragraph gives an account of a Darwin man who shot dead a neighbour and injured a woman before killing himself. What, you may ask, would annoy a man enough to cause him to take a shotgun to his neighbours? Good question. The article tells us that he was 'sick of all the noise' because his neighbours were playing their country music too loud.

Now I have to be honest. I sincerely hope that when I finally get launched into eternity, it is over a bigger deal than the back fence or the neighbour's loud music. I just think I would feel downright embarrassed if St Peter asked how come I had arrived at the Pearly Gates and I had to tell him I had a heart attack arguing with my neighbour about his tree growing over my fence, or I shot myself because the music next door was too loud!

Unfortunately, the human capacity to make little deals into big deals appears to be remarkably robust.

Paul refuses to be caught like this. To be fair, being in prison, facing a possible death sentence, and having other preachers trying to create dissension does sound pretty important. But Paul simply hands it over to God since he, personally, can do nothing about it anyway. He refuses to let it cost him sleep. He refuses to add it to his personal load.

A caveat. This is not to imply that nothing is a big deal. Some things in our lives are clearly monumental in their consequences, and we will inevitably respond by being emotionally overloaded at times. The point here is more directed at our tendency to treat many things as big deals, to feel completely overloaded because of the way we view them, to lose sleep, even to become ill because of them – when the truth is that they are something we will not even remember a week later!

Our tendency to make little deals into big deals creates stress and overload.

It would be marvellously therapeutic for each of us to ask ourselves ten times each day: Is this really a big deal? Do I have to get myself upset over this? Or can I adjust my perspective, remind myself that God is in control of even this, and get onto more productive pathways of functioning?

There is something here for each of us, but we have to introduce it into our experience. We have to begin, with God's help, to take some action on it, so that it becomes a tool in our lives, helping us to not carry the kinds of emotional loads we so often choose to carry. Undertaking this has great potential for a dramatic alteration in the experience of our inner world.

Letting Go of the Past

In Philippians 3:13–14 Paul writes:

> *Beloved, I do not consider that I have made it [his goal] my own; but this one thing I do: forgetting what lies behind and straining forward to what lies ahead, I press on toward the goal for the prize of the heavenly call of God in Christ Jesus.*

The truth is that Paul had a pretty rugged past! It was not pretty by any standards. He had been a zealous persecutor of Christians, and he seems to have been the central figure in the killing of the first Christian martyr, Stephen. He had certainly pursued Christians in Jerusalem and beyond, broken up families, thrown people into gaol. It is likely that others had been killed, and certainly large numbers suffered as a result of his actions. It is even likely that, after his conversion, there were still people imprisoned by the Jewish authorities as a result of his former way of life. It seems reasonable to ask: How come he is not overloaded with guilt for everything he has done to wreck the lives of other Christians?

While we do not have a direct answer to that question, we have some helpful information. In Galatians 1:17–18 we learn that after his conversion, and before he got going as a Christian preacher, Paul spent time down in Arabia, possibly up to three years. We can assume that this was his time of studying the Scriptures and sorting out his past before God. Somehow in this period he was able to receive an assurance of forgiveness, and since he could not undo the past, he determined that with God's help he would put it behind him and press on towards the goal of fulfilling his new calling in Christ. There was no other useful thing that he could do.

It is out of this context that he talks about 'forgetting what lies behind'.

A large part of the unnecessary load that many people carry is *regret for the past*. They wish, with all their heart, that they had not done some action or been involved in some situation. Unable to either change the past or let it go, they drag their regret with them into every new day. Added to the rest of their load, this not infrequently becomes overload.

'Leaving the past behind' is not a light or superficial thing. If our past involves actions that we can correct, then in order to be at peace we need to correct them. And we need to seek God's forgiveness. On the other hand, if there is nothing we can do to change the past, then we need to bring the situation honestly before God, preferably in the presence of a trusted friend, and seek his forgiveness. And then we need to receive, and live in, that gracious forgiveness.

Experiencing Forgiveness

As always, in order for our inner world to be transformed, we need to *experience* the truth of God's forgiveness so that we can leave the past behind.

Marlene struggled with acute depression, rooted in a profound sense of guilt. A young Christian woman of around twenty-five years of age, she had become pregnant by her boyfriend. Then, after a traumatic time trying to decide what to do, she allowed herself to be persuaded to have an abortion. She was quite inconsolable when she came to our clinic. It seemed virtually impossible to penetrate the shell of self-hatred and denigration that she carried.

Naturally it was not long before I (Cliff) found myself talking about the grace of God and his ready forgiveness for those who came to him in penitence. Her mind knew it, but there seemed no way she could receive it. We actually spent time preparing for a session of confession, and Marlene made her prayer before God. But she still walked out of the office gripped with regret and self-loathing for her action. I remember feeling quite powerless, not knowing what more I could do.

To my surprise, a completely different young woman walked into my office the next week. She was smiling and looked completely different. She told me her story.

A night or two after our session, she was driving home on one of the highways out of the city when her little car simply stopped. No matter what she did, it refused to go again. She got out and a young man helped her push it around a corner into a side street. It was after 7.00 pm and she wondered what she could do. Then she noticed the name of the street she was in, and remembered that years before she had attended a church just down that street a little. *Perhaps there'll be someone at the church who can help me,* she thought.

She walked down to the church and, sure enough, there was a small group of people having a meeting there. She interrupted their Bible study to ask if someone could help her. The leader told her they would be glad to help, but asked if she would

Perfection in our own strength not only brings stress and overload but leaves no room for God's grace.

mind if they finished their study first. So Marlene sat, brought there for an appointment arranged by God.

The study was on the life of Paul and the theme was something like 'Shadows of the Past'. It focused on Paul's destructive life before coming to Christ. The group discussed how Paul had been responsible for the deaths of Christians, had thrown people into prison and broken up families. He could not undo what had been done. One option before him was to be overwhelmed by guilt and simply crawl into a hole, despising himself forever. Satan would have been pleased by such an outcome! What Paul in fact chose to do was to receive God's forgiveness, then let his past go in order to move on.

As she listened, this became a sacred moment for Marlene. With tears streaming down her face, she knew that God had brought her to hear this message. That night she *experienced* his forgiveness. She was able at last to let go of the load of guilt she had been carrying.

Sometimes the overload of regret comes from guilt over

something we have done that was wrong. Sometimes it comes from guilt about something we feel we should have done and failed to do. Whatever it is, the remedy ultimately lies in dealing with it before God and leaving the past behind.

The hardest struggle for people in this area frequently comes from the fact that they have not *experienced* forgiveness. They have the required understanding, the head knowledge, but they long for an overwhelming experience – a moment when, with tears streaming down their face, they *know* that they are forgiven. They long for the kind of moment that Marlene experienced.

Unfortunately, we do not have control over this. This is territory that is in God's sovereign hands. Our only useful task, having asked God for forgiveness, is to accept by faith that it is ours, *whether we have an emotional experience or not*. Our trust at this point has to be in the certainty of God's word, whether our feelings have been engaged or not. Perhaps we honour God even more when we trust him even though we have not seen or felt!

Progress, not Perfection

In Philippians 3 Paul outlines another principle that underlies the development of a renewed inner world. Having spoken about his desire 'to know Christ, and the power of his resurrection and the sharing of his sufferings' (verse 10), he goes on: 'Not that I have already obtained this or have already reached the goal; but I press on to make it my own, because Christ Jesus has made me his own' (verse 12).

Paul is frankly acknowledging here that he has not yet made it. He still has more to learn, more to do, more to grow in. Nor does he seem to be overwhelmed with guilt about this. Rather, he seems to have a reasonably healthy perspective on it. He will press on, but he absolutely is not going to sit in the middle of the road and lament the fact that he is not yet perfect. He will make progress his goal, and let that continue to grow him forward. Perfection is somewhere further down the track, but it certainly is not his goal. It will have to wait. The absence of it at this point in time is simply not his main concern.

One of the biggest sources of overload that arises in people's inner worlds is the tendency to have incredibly tough personal expectations. They expect too much of themselves! Such people are often perfectionists.

Perfectionists are people whose inner worlds contain rules about how things *should* be done. As they have grown up, somehow these folk have taken into themselves a set of demands that they have to live by. These inner demands can include everything from 'rules' about the one and only correct way to do certain tasks, to inflexible expectations of themselves to always do tasks perfectly. Sometimes they carry a demand that they must always be the best in everything they do. Anything less than perfection is viewed as a failure. And they berate themselves, feeling guilty and depressed, if they do not achieve at the standard required by their inner demands.

Eric was in the top echelon of management in his company. As a known Christian, he felt it was an important part of his witness to always be available to hear the complaints and gripes of a thousand workers, and to try to mediate and help them get things sorted out. Apparently they liked the idea, and a lot of them took him up on his availability. The problem was that he could not get his own work done, so he spent much of the weekend catching up. It worked for a few years, but when he came into our office he was burned out and depressed.

Eric was convinced that he was doing what God expected. For him it was fundamental that God would expect him *always* to be available. He had to do this perfectly or he was letting God down severely. It took him a while to understand that God did not, in fact, expect perfect performance from him in this area. When he came to see that Jesus himself set boundaries and did not try to meet everyone's expectations perfectly, he was gradually able to make the necessary changes to his inner world.

Yvette was an extremely bright MA student in a Counselling Psychology programme at a university where one of us was teaching. The programme was very selective. Only ten students out of an application pool of around 115 had been chosen, and Yvette was one of them.

However, Yvette was also a perfectionist in her self-expectations. There was no flexibility at all built into her understanding of what constituted a fulfilling and successful way of life. When Yvette found that her results in some of the courses placed her as the *second* best student, she was literally plunged into a suicidal depression. She, too, required ongoing counselling in order to be able to readjust her overly-rigid inner world and get on with her study and her life.

For our inner world to be transformed, we need to experience the truth of God's forgiveness.

Perfectionistic demands prevent people from trying out new behaviours. Because the inner rule says 'you must not fail', it becomes a terrifying exercise to have to write an essay in a completely new topic area or to try out a new skill. The person who is condemned to have to do something *perfectly*, when they have never done it before, will often find reasons not to proceed with their attempt.

Irrational Beliefs

Perfectionists operate with some kind of inner belief that goes something like this: 'I must be thoroughly competent, adequate and successful in everything I do, or else it's terrible and awful, and I'm a failure, and doomed to feel really bad about myself for the rest of my life.'

Albert Ellis, who first wrote about these inner beliefs, called them Irrational Beliefs.[1] They are irrational because they are simply not true. Yet the trouble is, they feel true! Usually the belief has been held for so long the person feels an inner conviction of its validity. If it is to be changed, some of Ellis' suggestions will be helpful.

First, we have to learn to *dispute* them, to argue against them in our minds, pointing out their falseness. We have to do this forcefully and frequently, with considerable energy and commitment.

Next, we have to *replace* them with rational beliefs, followed by rational conclusions. You will notice that the irrational belief statement above is actually made up of an irrational belief ('I must be thoroughly competent, adequate and successful in everything I do'), followed by an irrational conclusion ('or else it's terrible and awful, and I'm a failure, doomed to feel really bad about myself for the rest of my life'). These irrational parts need to be deleted and new programming put in to replace them.

One of the best ways to do this, according to Ellis, is to *replace demands with preferences*. A demand is expressed as 'I must/should/ought'. A preference is expressed as 'I would prefer that/It would be nice if/I would really like to'. Such preferences are rational, and they are vastly more flexible than the rigid demands we tend to live with.

If we were to change the perfectionist's demands to preferences, and his or her irrational conclusion to a rational conclusion, the belief might look something like this: 'It would be nice if I were always thoroughly competent, adequate and successful in everything I do, but the truth is that's not likely. And it's also true that I can live a perfectly fulfilling and worthwhile life even if I occasionally make a mess of something.'

For Paul, that is pretty much what he believes. He keeps his eyes focused on the big picture: 'Am I making progress? Can I learn from that experience, and so do better next time?' He is not too worried about apparent 'failure'. For him the only real failure lies in not trying, and that he will never do. He is committed to pressing on – to progress, not perfection!

Resting in Christ

To justify their perfectionism, people sometimes quote Matthew 5:48, which is usually translated something like this: 'Be perfect, just as your heavenly Father is perfect.'

Now the one thing that this verse cannot really mean is that we are to strive for perfection in our own strength, on the basis that this is a possible and realistic goal. If it were possible, then we would have no need for Christ's death and God's redemptive grace. If it were possible, either before becoming Christians or after, to live in sinless perfection, then we would have no ongoing need of grace.

We are impressed, as others are, by the fact that the verse asks us to 'be' perfect. We get it all wrong when we turn it into a command to 'do' perfectly. The only way we know of 'being' perfect is to continue to receive the forgiving grace of God and the imparted righteousness of Christ. Matthew 5:48 is an instruction about *being*, not *doing*.

Perhaps the best understanding of the call to 'be perfect' is to see it as God's call to us to *rest* in perfection. We know of no other perfection than Christ. This, then, is a call to us to rest in Christ, to dwell in him, to draw from him. In the area of our doing, Paul's word is wisdom. It reminds us that God calls us to progress in our living; he does not call us to an impossible standard of perfection.

Many of the overstressed people who show up at our clinic are working this one the wrong way round. Their goal is 'perfection, not progress'. Sometimes they are clearly making progress in life and there is evidence of improvement and healing, but somehow this is all discounted because they are not perfect. Frankly, it is a tragedy.

Paul knows this. He is not perfect, but then he does not fool himself that achieving perfectly is what God expects of him. In the area of achievement he defines the important thing as 'making progress'. And that is where he puts his effort: 'I press on...'

Notes
1. See *A New Guide to Rational Living* by A. Ellis and R. Harper. Ellis's concepts have much to offer, although he is quite anti-Christian in much of his writing.

 # SUMMARY

■ We all live out of a 'reality' that we have constructed as a result of the experiences we have gone through in growing up.

■ The reality we live out of is an imperfect representation of Reality. It does not correspond exactly with anyone else's reality, and it is made up of emotional, cognitive, somatic and kinesthetic elements, some of which are conscious and some of which are unconscious.

■ Because our reality is constructed, it can be deconstructed – and reconstructed so that it becomes a more helpful approximation of Reality.

■ As humans we often view relatively unimportant events as 'big deals', and this frequently adds unnecessarily to our sense of overload. We have to develop our capacity to view things with a more balanced perspective.

■ Holding on to regrets about the past only increases our sense of overload. God has made provision for us to be freed from this. Our task is to simply avail ourselves of this provision.

■ We need to let go of inner world demands for us to perform perfectly, and reconstruct our value around learning to rejoice in progress.

Your personal Overload Check-up

1. To what extent am I a person who tends to turn little, relatively unimportant life-events into 'big deals' that cause me to stress out and feel overloaded?

_____

_____

2. Ask friends or family members about how they see you in regard to this. Do they see you as a person who over-reacts, someone who turns molehills into mountains?

_____

_____

3. If I *am* a person who tends to see every broken shoelace, every annoying circumstance, as a personal affront, and so choose to let myself be upset by it, where did I learn to do this? From whom? How has this pattern of reacting affected my relationships with other people over the years? How has it affected my stress levels?

_____

_____

4. Have I learned to let go of the past, to put my regrets aside, to forgive myself and others? Or do I still carry bitterness, guilt or unforgiveness towards others? If so, how has this affected my relationships, my achievements and/or my health over the years?

_____

_____

_____

5. Is there something that I still need to do in order to 'leave the past behind'? If so, what is the first step? Who could I talk to in order to get started?

_____

_____

_____

_____

 **ACTION**

We have found it helpful to ask people to read over the Parable of the Prodigal Son (Luke 15:11–32) every day for a month, asking God to speak to them about his character and his attitude to them. Somehow in the process of allowing this parable to marinate through the inner world, changes often seem to occur, and people are freed from unhelpful and unrealistic self-demands. Perhaps this is something for you to undertake over the next month.

Chapter Ten

Renewing Your Inner World — II

Foundations

The inner world is the world of our attitudes and inner experience, conscious and unconscious, which has been shaped by our growing up. Because none of us grew up in a perfect external world, and because none of us had perfect parents or other significant people in our lives (even though they might have been, overall, very positive influences), we all end up with 'inner-world static'. We all have some attitudes, beliefs, emotional responses, somatic and kinesthetic responses that do not serve us well in terms of our tendency to overload ourselves.

Yesterday a businessman came to our clinic. He was a deeply committed Christian, active in his local church. He had risen close to the top in his management area, largely by virtue of his ability and the long hours of work he had been putting in. Just over fifty years old, he had suddenly 'hit the wall', showing all the signs of classic burnout, with depressive symptoms – no physical or emotional energy, cynical about the motives of his employers, no pleasure in things that had once given him pleasure, disturbed eating and sleeping, a feeling of bleakness over all his functioning.

As we talked he shared that, from both his parents, he had been given the message that 'good enough' simply did not exist. Out of their inner-world distortions they had conveyed to him that he 'should' this and he 'should' that, to the point where his life was largely controlled by 'shoulds' and 'musts' and 'oughts'. It was this relentless, inner-world system of attitudes that had largely caused him to work so hard and long, until the overload simply exhausted him emotionally and physically.

We constantly need corrective wisdom for our inner world. We never get past the need for a work of renewal to be done here. And the good news is that this is exactly what God wants to do in us.

An Attitude of Rejoicing

In our need for inner-world renewal, once again Paul, in his letter to the Philippians, gives us guidance. 'Finally, my brothers and sisters, rejoice in the Lord' (Philippians 3:1). He repeats the instruction a little later: 'Rejoice in the Lord always; again I will say, Rejoice' (Philippians 4:4).

The message is clear. Paul directs us to adopt an attitude of rejoicing – always! This is directly related to our unloading the overload. Somehow the load is much easier to carry if we can just get our hearts into rejoice mode.

In a way this is weird stuff. We wonder if it is really possible. We recognise that life is tough, and there are a lot of lousy things that happen. Is it realistic to suggest that we should adopt an attitude of rejoicing always? How can we rejoice if we lose our job or our health is packing it in? How can we rejoice if we cannot pay the bills or there is no money for Christmas presents for the children? Has Paul finally lost it? Has he been so long in prison that his mind is starting to play tricks on him?

No, Paul has not sprung a leak. Perhaps more than almost anyone else, he knows the reality of tough times in the service of Christ. He knows about stonings and whippings, about cold and hunger. He knows about loneliness and fear. He knows about being shipwrecked, lost in the ocean, longing for land. In a way, the guidance here links in with the 'big deal' attitude expressed in Philippians 1:18. Paul is simply acknowledging that, if the deep foundations in life are in place, then even these sufferings and trials cannot ultimately defeat God's purposes for us. And in *that* we can rejoice!

We do not rejoice *because* bad things happen to us. We rejoice because God is in control of our life, even *when* bad things happen to us. Run that again in your mind. We rejoice *because God*…!

Most of us know someone who has developed this positive attitude to a reasonable degree. I (Cliff) think of Charles, an ageing Scottish gentleman who was in our church for many years. Whatever the weather, he would always greet me with a smile. In his broad Scottish accent it was always a 'grand day, m'boy', and he was always feeling 'tip top!' You could not help but feel uplifted by his seemingly unstoppable attitude of rejoicing.

Or I think of old Mr Blyth, long since dead but a significant member in the church in Wagga when I was growing up. I was just a boy, but he left a deep impression on me because he saw life through eyes that rejoiced in God's goodness. My recollection is that he brought an attitude of thankfulness and joy with him whenever he visited our place. He seemed to use the word 'wonderful' a lot. The day was 'wonderful'; life was 'wonderful'. It's a good word – *wonder-full*.

I think of my mother, now in a nursing home with Alzheimer's Disease, who nevertheless lives a life still largely marked by thankfulness. Most of the time 'everyone is so good' to her, and 'we've got a lot to be thankful for'. She never sees a tree without expressing her thankfulness to God for trees. 'Aren't trees wonderful!' is indelibly recorded in her inner world. Even with Alzheimer's she is usually a delight to be with.

This kind of attitude of rejoicing is not something that comes easily or naturally to us. Quite the opposite; we have to grow it. We have to practise! When I visit mum in the nursing home I see some extremely bitter elderly folk. I am not surprised they do not seem to have many visitors. I recognise that they got this way by practising being bitter as they encountered tough times in the journey of their lives. And I remind myself that, right now, I am preparing myself to be either a bitter person or a rejoicing person when I make it to the nursing home. It is a sobering thought. I want someone to visit me. I want someone to push my wheelchair!

That thought reinforces for me the wisdom of what Paul is telling us here. 'Make it your practice to rejoice. Remind yourself that God's sovereign purposes for you can never be defeated. Drink in his goodness from the beauty of creation around you, and rejoice!'

But the benefits are not just future. Essentially they are here for us every day. If we daily remind ourselves of the blessings in our lives, if we will work at developing this attitude of rejoicing, the load will be lighter – now!

Positive Loading

In Philippians 4:8 Paul instructs his readers on another important principle that is intimately related to handling overload. He writes:

> Finally, beloved, whatever is true, whatever is honourable, whatever is just, whatever is pure, whatever is pleasing, whatever is commendable, if there is any excellence and if there is anything worthy of praise, think about these things.

These words remind us that we have to be proactive in ensuring that what we take into our minds is not simply the rubbish served up by the world, but is a diet of positive, ennobling material. If we simply sit back and allow ourselves to be mentally 'fed' by the society around us, we will end up with a massive overdose of attitude-pollutants. And they will significantly add to our feelings of overload.

Our media, electronic and print, are predominantly focused on 'what is wrong'. Any day of the week, the TV news reports wars, massacres, acts of violence, political controversy, disagreement, character assassination, sleaze, and a host of other kinds of negative material. Very little time is given to positive, uplifting reports.

We are not in the dark about the impact of all this on human functioning. We learned that repeatedly seeing aggressive behaviour modelled by others, either live or on film, increases the likelihood that we will incorporate aggressive behaviour into our repertoire.

If you stay within life's safety zones, you will never attempt anything that you are not familiar with.

What we take into our minds affects the way we live.

When we feed on a regular diet of lies, deception, violence and stories of people being used and abused, something changes inside us. The change is frequently subtle, and there are some who argue that no such change occurs. However, there is good research evidence to suggest that, cumulatively, we lose our distinctive human capacities – the ability to empathise, compassion, the capacity to consider others ahead of ourselves, self-discipline and the capacity to delay gratification. We are more prone to cynicism and discouragement, and we lose our natural capacity for joy and relaxation.

If we live a busy life, a life with many demands, then we cannot afford to let the surrounding culture simply load our minds with uncensored junk. In fact, we need to do our own censoring. We need to eliminate a lot of the unedifying, intellectual junk food that is served up in movies, videos, women's magazines, men's magazines and other media. Instead, we need to find ways of ensuring that we provide a diet for ourselves of healthy, wholesome cognitive material, so that our minds run on what is positive rather than what is negative.

What, in fact, can we do to ensure that we are taking in positive material, in line with Paul's advice? Consider a range of options.

One important word of warning needs to be included here. Christian bookshops have many self-help books that integrate biblical understanding with some of the useful understandings

- Regular reading of Scripture, with a focus on the character of God and the certainty of his eternal purposes, is certainly a good start.

- Read good books. While this could include everything from classics to well-written suspense novels, it will not contain books that are loaded with gratuitous sex and violence, or themes that are constantly dark and depressing.

- Listen to good music, music that uplifts, refreshes and focuses your mind on what is good. This may well include contemporary praise and worship music, favourite hymns, classical music and jazz. Check the effect to make sure that what you listen to *is* a positive influence in your mind.

- Read devotional books, especially books with a positive emphasis. Christian bookshops are full of excellent material that is written to lift the spirit and provide useful guidance.

- Read Christian biographies. Read the lives of great heroes of the Christian faith such as John Wesley, George Whitfield, William Carey, C.T. Studd, Henry Martyn, St Francis, George Muller, Charles Finney and Hudson Taylor, or contemporaries such as Billy Graham, Mother Teresa and Joni Erikson Tada. Their lives are real and include much hardship, but their stories bear testimony to the goodness and faithfulness of God.

- Put positive-message posters on your walls, or similar messages in a frame on your desk, so that your mind is quietly absorbing their message on a constant basis.

- Make sure that you include activities in your life that put you in contact with things that are beautiful, positive and good. Activities such as relaxing exercise, bushwalking, drives in the countryside, visits to art galleries and botanical gardens, and attending good plays and music concerts could come into this category.

we have from psychology. These are often very helpful.

However, it can be a trap to become over-occupied with reading these kind of books. Limit your reading in this area, so that you do not become overly-focused on introspection and 'sorting out all my problems'. If we take in more than a healthy balance of such material, the danger is that we can start to bury ourselves in our problems, failings, struggles and imperfections once more. This is certainly not what Paul had in mind when he directed us to focus on those things that are good and true and pure.

Learning to be Content

The last instruction that we take from Paul's letter to the Philippians is from the final chapter. Paul shares here a secret with the folk at Philippi when he says:

> *I have learned to be content with whatever I have. I know what it is to have little, and I know what it is to have plenty. In any and all circumstances I have learned the secret of being well-fed and of going hungry, of having plenty and of being in need.*
>
> (Philippians 4:11–12)

The most important word here is the word 'learned'. Paul repeats it twice. His use of this word tells us that his capacity to adjust his inner world so that external circumstances do not overwhelm him was not something that just happened. He did not acquire this capacity by genetic transmission, nor was it a fortuitous gift from the gods. He *learned* it. He 'went to school' for it. The 'school', of course, was the range of life experiences that he went through, and the practice that he had in drawing on God's grace to sustain him in those experiences. By encountering life in its full range of pleasant and difficult aspects, and by drawing strength from God, he learned contentment.

A short while ago, I (Cliff) received a phone call from my son to say that he had just lost his wallet. There was over a hundred dollars in it, plus his licence and a few plastic cards. Any dad worth his salt would find it hard not to deliver a lecture under these circumstances, but, you know, I think I must be getting old. I can recall three lost wallets over the past four years in our family, plus a stolen handbag, so I feel like I have been to school on this one. And I think I am learning that this, too, is just a piece of life, and another opportunity to draw on the grace of God. So I did not do my block or deliver a lecture. Instead I listened a bit, then said a prayer for the wallet's safe return. Perhaps, under the tuition of God, I am learning to be content, instead of chafing over things that I have no immediate power to change. It's an encouraging thought.

Often we would prefer to avoid learning contentment because it is inconvenient and may even be deeply painful. Many people try to stay in life's safety zones, never attempting anything that they are not completely familiar with. They work hard to protect themselves, to not take risks, to be in full control, to look after Number One. Some of this may be wisdom. Too much of it, however, is an avoiding of the full range of life, an avoiding of the opportunity to learn contentment. Not a lot of contentment comes out of obsessive, self-protective living.

Normal life gives us the opportunity to learn contentment. But to do well we have to draw on the strength that God provides through Jesus. How else will we learn contentment in a world where so much is driven by consumerism and an out-of-control proliferation of enticements to seek after every new bit of technical gadgetry?

The absence of contentment is a significant factor in our feeling of overload. Without contentment in our inner world, we are driven, we are restless, we are tempted to do more, spend more, seek more. If, with God's help, we commit ourselves to learning contentment, we will carry with us something precious in the management of overload.

SUMMARY

■ Paul advises us to adopt an attitude of rejoicing – always! While at one level this may seem unrealistic, Paul is obviously not talking out of a sheltered life, but out of one that has been profoundly populated with times of struggle and suffering. The key to adopting this attitude lies in reminding ourselves of the unconquerable benevolence of God towards us, so that his purposes for us will never ultimately be defeated.

■ Our inner world will be overloaded with negative content if we simply leave it to society around us to provide for our inner experiencing. Once again, Paul's instructions are helpful. He urges us to practise positive loading. We are encouraged to consciously and intentionally make sure that we take a regular diet of positive and encouraging material into our experiencing. This will come out of *doing* things that build in positive experience, and *taking in through our senses* a range of positive material. This is not a recommendation to avoid the tough aspects of life, but a recognition that as humans we must have a balance in our lives, preferably one in which positive material is dominant.

■ Paul also encourages us to be learners of contentment. He shares with us the fact that he has learned the secret of contentment, not out of hot-house living, but out of the storms and struggles of his life. Handled well, the tough experiences of our lives can teach us contentment too.

Your personal Overload Check-up

1. Who do I personally know that seems to live out of a position of inner joy?

_____

_____

2. To what extent am I a person who has taken on board Paul's advice to 'rejoice in all things'? What holds me back from being more joyful?

_____

_____

3. In life's difficult situations, how am I doing in reminding myself that God is still in control? Can I think of a situation recently where I have tried to rejoice, even though the external events did not seem so positive?

_____

_____

4. What do I tend to soak my mind in through my reading? What do I tend to view? What effects does this have on me?

_____

_____

5. How content am I as a person? What were my parents like on this score? To what extent have I taken on their attitude of discontentment or contentment?

_____

_____

Chapter Eleven

God's Rhythm of Life

Foundations

In this day of milliseconds and micro-units, it is hard to conceive that there is a kind of living that centres around a relaxing rhythm of life – a lifestyle where time is a satisfying process, not a devouring enemy to be subdued. We call this 'God's rhythm of life', the peaceful pacing of life after the patterns of God.

Shalom is the Hebrew word for the inner harmony, or 'integratedness', that comes from living within this rhythm. Loosely translated, *shalom* is the peace of God. All we have written in

Enjoying God's rhythm of life makes the work flow with less strain.

this book is really intended to introduce you to this kind of living – a living which gives *shalom*.

God's rhythm is a structural element of life, perhaps the basic building block. Without being too mystical about it, we would see God's rhythm of life as implanted deep within all of his creation. The seasons move to a rhythm, new warmth and life emerging from the cold sleep of winter. Plants produce their fruit then wither and die, only to sprout again as the sun returns to germinate their seed. Animals and humans are born, live out their full flush of youth, grow old and pass away, only to be replaced by a following generation.

The writer of Ecclesiastes describes this rhythm in part:

> *A generation goes, and a generation comes,*
> *but the earth remains forever.*
> *The sun rises and the sun goes down,*
> *and hurries to the place where it rises.*
> *The wind blows to the south,*
> *and goes around to the north;*
> *round and round goes the wind,*
> *and on its circuits the wind returns.*
> *All streams run to the sea,*
> *but the sea is not full;*
> *to the place where the stream flow,*
> *there they continue to flow.* (Ecclesiastes 1:4–7)

Learning to live God's rhythm is a process that we enter into little by little, and as we do so we appropriate more of his *shalom*. The basic elements of God's rhythm are laid out for us in the first chapter of the Bible.

Evening and Morning

Eugene Peterson, in an article entitled 'The Pastor's Sabbath',[1] calls our attention to God's creative rhythm, and no one has described it better. Peterson calls it the 'genesis rhythm', but we might think of it just as God's rhythm. Peterson notes that God instituted some patterns when he created our world. First of all, we need to understand how God's rhythm works.

The first element of the rhythm that produces *shalom* is recorded in the account of the first day of Creation.

> *Then God said, 'Let there be light', and there was light. And God saw the light, that it was good; and God divided the light from the darkness. God called the light Day, and the darkness He called Night. So the evening and the morning were the first day.* (Genesis 1:35, NKJV)

God continues his creative acts, and then we are told: 'so the evening and the morning were the second day.' Once again God is involved in creating, in working, and then the rhythm repeats: 'So the evening and the morning were the third day.' More creative activity… 'So the evening and the morning were the fourth day'… God working… 'So the evening and the morning were the fifth day'… God creating… 'So the evening and the morning were the sixth day.'

The first significant thing that Peterson draws to our attention is the unexpected juxtaposition of evening and morning in the daily rhythm. We would most likely describe the rhythm of our daily life as 'morning and evening'. Why is God's day, God's creative rhythm, described as 'evening and morning' instead? What are we being told here?

The first thing to note is that during the evening, when we are sleeping, we are not in charge. We are not labouring. We are not doing. We are just resting. God, however, is at work. He is energising our bodies and minds. Proteins and chemicals are being changed into a supply of energy. If we thought 'the evening' was dead time, lost time, wasted time, we would completely miss the point. A work of preparation is going on inside us and in the world, without our conscious effort.

Regular worship and times with God is the secret of unloading the overload.

This is an implanted, secret work of God, and it is preparatory to *our* labour, which begins in 'the morning'. When we start our labour, it is firmly grounded in God's preparatory action within us and around us. We begin, dependent on his grace. 'Evening, then morning.'

The other way round would put our efforts and labour first, as though it were some intrinsic capability we had that enabled us to achieve. God's work would be relegated to restoring us after we had drained ourselves in serving him. But 'evening and morning' makes it clear that our labour proceeds out of God's preparatory activity.

When God prepares us, the work flows with less strain. It is his work. When we take the other path – when we get launched in our own strength, trusting God to renew us – somehow we have it back to front, and we live with a much greater danger of overload.

'Evening and morning' also reminds us that every day we awake into a world in which God has been active. We are not the crucial factor we sometimes think we are. Surprisingly, we are actually not Managing Directors of the universe! It is *his* world. We awake into a world which he has created and experience his unearned grace again. Grace has gone before us. God has prepared both us and the world, and now he calls us into his world – to share his work, to enjoy his gifts, to praise his creative acts.

The Artist has been at work. The world is his canvas. Will we stop and look? Will we acknowledge the wonder of his marvellous creation? Or will we just stumble into our mouse-wheel activity, as though we were the first here, as though he were not ahead of us, as though everything depended on us? 'Evening and morning' – God, then me. No, that's not quite right. 'Evening and morning' – God, then God-and-me!

Understanding this, and living in the awareness of it, is the first building-block in God's rhythm of life. He has gone before me into all that I seek to do. He has prepared me in ways beyond my conscious awareness. All of my life is his, and when I go into my daily work, into business meetings, ordinary tasks, people-relating, he has prepared me and goes before me.

The Sabbath

The second part of God's rhythm that we see in Genesis 1 is described at the end of God's creative action. The sixth day has ended and now the seventh day has come. Now there is a change to the rhythm: 'And on the seventh day God finished the work that he had done, and he rested on the seventh day from all the work that he had done' (Genesis 2:2).

Eugene Peterson again is helpful:

> Sabbath extrapolates this basic, daily rhythm into the larger context of the month. The turning of the earth on its axis gives us the basic two-beat rhythm, evening/morning. The moon in its orbit introduces another rhythm, the twenty-eight day month, marked by four phases of seven days each. It is this larger rhythm, the rhythm of the seventh day, that we are commanded to observe.
>
> Sabbath-keeping presumes the daily rhythm, evening/morning – we can hardly avoid stopping our work each night, as fatigue and sleep overtake us. But the weekly rhythm demands deliberate action. Otherwise we can go on working on the seventh day, especially if things are gaining momentum. Sabbath-keeping often feels like an interruption, an interference with our routines. It challenges assumptions we gradually build up that our daily work is indispensable in making the world go.
>
> But then we find the Sabbath is not an interruption but a stronger rhythmic measure that confirms and extends the basic beat. Every seventh day a deeper note is struck – an enormous gong whose deep sounds reverberate under and over and round the daily percussions evening/morning, evening/morning, evening/morning; creation honoured and contemplated, redemption remembered and shared.

It is true. We have no option but to observe the two-beat rhythm of evening/morning (although we can lose much of its significance by thinking of it as morning/evening). But we can easily be seduced into thinking that we do not need to stop one day in seven. Perhaps, as Peterson observes, this is why God *commanded* that we observe the Sabbath, rather than simply suggesting it!

What is the significance of this one-day-in-seven rest that we call the Sabbath?

Fairly clearly, it is not the importance of the day itself. One day will serve as well as another. Saturday or Wednesday or any other day – no big deal! Paul makes this clear in Romans 14:56. No, it is not the particular day.

The issue is the cessation of labour in order to rest and be renewed. Once again we are back in grace-territory. This is a day set aside for us to stop our busy-ness, to follow the model of God who rested on the seventh day. It is the second part of the God-rhythm. We begin our work in grace – evening/morning. And we finish our week of work in grace – observing a Sabbath. The rhythm begins and ends in the grace of God.

The writer to the Hebrews urges us to be aware that 'a sabbath rest still remains for the people of God... Let us therefore make every effort to enter that rest, so that no one may fall through such disobedience as theirs' (Hebrews 4:9,11). He is reminding us here that the withdrawing, resting rhythm that is Sabbath is still active. It is for us. It is part of God's rhythm of life, and it brings us into harmony with God. It is a reminder to live in grace. It gifts us with *shalom*.

Getting Practical

But how do we go about living in God's rhythm of life? What are the practical implications?

The first one, of course, is adjusting our minds. When we start to line our lives up with this rhythm, we begin by acknowledging that our lives begin and end in God's grace. Everything we do depends for its worthwhileness on his preparatory activity in us and in our world. And after we have done anything at all – secular work, spiritual service, whatever – we have nowhere to go but to 'Sabbath' in his grace and be renewed.

This is a powerful paradigm shift for those of us who are

driven. We carry the sense so easily that we are important, that our work *must* be done. Not so. God reigns. And he calls us to live lightly, dependent not on our big efforts but on his grace. It is a way of thinking that carries great freedom for us.

But, even more practically, consider the diagram which divides the time we spend in our lives into quadrants between **Urgent/Not Urgent** and **Important/Not Important**.

	IMPORTANT	NOT IMPORTANT
URGENT		
NOT URGENT		

What are the activities in your life that you would place in the Urgent/Important quadrant? Probably much of our life is spent here. We have to go to work to earn a living, so that is important, and it is also urgent. Our employer, or employees, expects us to be there. There are other tasks that clearly fit in here.

We also find ourselves spending quite a bit of time in the Urgent/Not Important quadrant. The time spent on doing stuff in this area is usually spent because someone else has expectations of us. They want us to finish something for them or help them with some task. In the grand scheme of life we do not actually see it as very important, but they have asked us and they require it. So we fill out another survey form or collect data on another project that will be filed in a dusty cabinet somewhere. We rush to buy the present that will not really be appreciated or stress out tidying the house before the guests arrive, saying things to each other that we are sorry about afterwards.

Urgent, but not really important. Think of what you would put here from your life.

Then we come to the Important/Not Urgent category. There are some clear activities to put in here. This is where *relationship* time goes. Time spent building friendships, time spent catching up with friends, time spent maintaining relationships. This is where we include sharing time between husband and wife, family time, parents doing stuff with their children. But it is also the category that takes in *recreation*. Regular exercise, sporting activity, enjoyable hobbies – activities that re-create and refresh us. Activities where we receive rather than give out.

You will perhaps not be surprised to note that the external changes we advocate in the first half of this book fit right into this third quadrant – important, but not necessarily urgent. When we clutter our lives up with Urgent stuff, this quadrant tends to be sacrificed. We plan to spend some time with our spouse – next week. We plan to re-contact those friends and have a good catch up – next week. We plan to get started on some regular exercise – next week. Unfortunately, right now we have just got too many demands, too much stuff on that is absolutely urgent. And so the Important gets put aside.

However, it is our contention that it is the Important stuff that makes our lives meaningful. If I am meeting my needs in this quadrant, then my life will have balance, and I will be better equipped to cope with the load that I carry in the Urgent areas. On the other hand, if my needs in the Important/Not Urgent quadrant are being put off because they are not Urgent, then I am much more susceptible to burn out. I am much more likely to break under the load. I am much more likely to find myself asking, 'What on earth am I doing this for?' The activities that make up this Important/Not Urgent quadrant actually give meaning to my life.

And so we come to the final quadrant – Not Important/Not Urgent. At first glance it would seem likely that there is nothing that should be put into this quadrant at all. If it is Not Important, and it is Not Urgent, why bother with it?

Perhaps it is time to note that these quadrants, as described here, represent time spent *the way the world would generally rate it*. Is there anything that our society would generally see as Not Important/Not Urgent that we would do well to give some time to?

Our contention is that there is. In fact, this is the quadrant where the rhythm of the Sabbath comes in. Much of our society would tend to see time used to rest as unproductive; time used to relax and enjoy God's goodness to us as pretty much a waste of time. Oh, they can handle the idea of relaxing, but appreciating God? Living in his grace? Nah! The consensus would count this as Not Important/Not Urgent – press the Delete button on it!

But it is our belief that this is the quadrant where we take time to appreciate the beauty in God's art gallery. All around us God's artistic handiwork is evident. The sad thing is that we rarely stop to smell the roses. We seldom stop to appreciate a jacaranda in bloom or a sunset poured out, golden, across the sky. When we get out into God's creation, when we take in the sights, sounds and smells of God's world, stopping to notice and to praise him from a full heart, we are being renewed.

This is the quadrant where we put on that CD or tape whose beauty or majesty touches emotions deep within. We stop and tune out the world, letting a fountain of sound wash over us, releasing, healing and restoring our soul.

This is the quadrant where we take time to read God's Love Letter to his creation, allowing sacred Scripture to do its deep work of healing and renewing. We stop and meditate. We think about the wonder of his love. We kneel quietly before him. We are moved to worship.

Perhaps no one has done a better job of describing the renewing moment of worship than Kenneth Grahame in his animal fantasy *Wind in the Willows*. In the chapter entitled 'The Piper at the Gates of Dawn', Grahame describes how Rat and Mole, moved by compassion for their friend Otter, whose young son Portly has gone missing, are unable to sleep. They decide to go out rowing on the river to help look for the young otter. On their errand of compassion, they become entranced by beautiful music played on pipes which draws them onwards, until they come into the presence of their god.

Then suddenly the Mole felt a great Awe fall upon him, an awe that turned his muscles to water, bowed his head, and rooted his feet to the ground. It was no panic terror – indeed he felt wonderfully at peace and happy – but it was an awe that smote and held him, and without seeing he knew it could only mean that some August Presence was very, very near. With difficulty he turned to look at his friend, and saw him at his side cowed, stricken, and trembling violently. And still there was utter silence in the populous bird-haunted branches around them; and still the light grew and grew.

Perhaps he would never have dared to raise his eyes, but that, though the piping was now hushed, the call and the summons seemed still dominant and imperious. He might not refuse, were Death himself waiting to strike him instantly, once he had looked with mortal eye on things rightly kept hidden. Trembling he obeyed, and raised his humble head; and then, in the utter clearness of the imminent dawn, while Nature, flushed with fullness of incredible colour, seemed to hold her breath for the even, he looked in the very eyes of the Friend and Helper...

'Rat!' he found breath to whisper, shaking. 'Are you afraid?'

'Afraid?' murmured the Rat, his eyes shining with unutterable love. 'Afraid! Of Him? O, never, never! And yet – and yet – O, Mole, I am afraid!'

Then the two animals, crouching to the earth, bowed their heads and did worship.

Sudden and magnificent, the sun's broad golden disc showed itself over the horizon facing them; and the first rays, shooting across the level water-meadows, took the animals full in the eyes and dazzled them. When they were able to look once more, the Vision had vanished, and the air was full of the carol of birds that hailed the dawn.[2]

The 'god' that the animals discover in this allegorical chapter is Pan, the god of the animals. But the writer is mirroring *our* experience of worship when he describes how they are affected:

There, in the place of the Vision, they find baby otter and are able to return the little fellow to his father, keeping vigil up by the weir.

Worship, public and personal – but especially personal – is renewing. It is perhaps the best expression of the intent behind God's creation of the Sabbath. This rhythmic break in our busy, activity-driven lives, this period of 'wasting time with God', finds its truest and most fulfilling expression in worship.

'Wasting time with God', learning to stop and enjoy his creation, learning to 'tune in' and worship him on a regular basis, is a great secret. This is central to God's rhythm of life. This produces *shalom*. This is spirit-renewal time. It is only Not Important and Not Urgent to those who are blind. To those who can see, it is the water of life! It makes all the difference.

More than anything, stopping our doing in order to worship and be renewed by God is the secret of unloading the overload.

Notes

1. Published in *Leadership*, Spring Quarter, 1985.
2. Kenneth Grahame, *The Wind in the Willows*. The original was published in 1908, but many editions are currently available. Ours is a Pavilion Classic published in 1997.

# SUMMARY

■ God has built a rhythm into his creation which is laid out for us in the first chapter of Genesis. It centres around two parts.

■ The first part is contained in the description of day as 'evening and morning', rather than the usual description we would use of 'morning and evening'. The significance of 'evening and morning' lies in the fact that our work, which starts in the morning, is already grounded in the preparatory work of God. We do what we do in a context of grace already provided. Once we understand this, and seek to live in the truth of it, we are freed from much of the personal burden-carrying that we otherwise fall into. All that we do is simply a joining in with God who has gone before us.

■ The second part of this God-rhythm emerges from the record that God rested on the seventh day, and that he commanded us to observe this rest. The particular day does not matter, but we *need* to give a priority to fitting this day of rest and renewal in.

■ In practical terms we need to look at how we split our time up in the four quadrants – Important/Urgent, Not Important/ Urgent, Important/Not Urgent and Not Important/Not Urgent. Analysis will soon reveal that, for the overloaded person, there is usually an imbalance. The Important/Not Urgent quadrant, one of the two that gives our lives most meaning, is frequently largely neglected.

■ Going further, we suggest that the quadrant viewed in our society as Not Important/Not Urgent may well be the most vital category. It is in this quadrant that we need to make a priority of 'wasting time with God' as a vital part of the way we use our time. While the value system of society might suggest that this is simply Not Important and Not Urgent, a deeper reality suggests that it, more than anything else, may be the lifeline that prevents overload. Time spent in worship is renewing; it centres us; it clarifies priorities; it changes us. It gives ultimate meaning to the load that each of us carries.

Your personal Overload Check-up

1. Do I tend to live without an adequate awareness of God's grace, his 'going-beforeness'? Do I tend to work as though 'God helps those who help themselves', forgetting the deep reality that his preparatory work precedes anything worthwhile that I might do?

_____

_____

2. If this is the case, what can I do to remind myself of the reality of God's grace? Have I lived in the awareness of this truth in times past but lost it? What do I need to do to rediscover it?

_____

3. How do I divide my time between the four quadrants mentioned in this chapter?

- What do I do that comes into the Important/Urgent category? What percentage of my time do I spend on these tasks?

  _____

- What do I do that comes into the category of Not Important/Urgent? What proportion of my time do I spend doing stuff in this category?

  _____

- What do I do that comes into the category of Important/Not Urgent? What proportion of my time do I spend in this category?

- What do I do that comes into the Not Important/Not Urgent category? Have I made time here for 'wasting time' in God's presence – for worship and adoration?

_____

4. What changes do I need to make to my use of time, as outlined in these four categories?

_____

_____

5. What is one practical step that I can begin with, as I seek to adjust my life so that I am more in tune with the rhythm that God has established?

_____

_____

Hang on...
I need to say
SOMETHING!

By Gillian Warren

This book could seriously change your relationship with your partner. Discover how to...

- *Resolve differences without a crisis*
- *Enjoy romance and intimacy again*
- *Learn new ways of saying 'I love you'*
- *Develop new skills for expressing yourself*

> *'An ideal book for engaged couples, partners, parents, and grandparents.'*

Gillian Warren and her husband Michael, hold residential weekends on their Sussex farm to encourage couples who are wanting to discover a more fulfilling relationship.

Illustrated with satirical cartoons by **Jacky Fleming**.

Hang on... I need to say something!
Gillian Warren
ISBN 1 899746 09 9
£5.99 UK

Available from your local Christian Bookshop.
In case of difficulty contact Gazelle Books,
Concorde House, Grenville Place, Mill Hill,
London NW7 3SA

Gazelle
BOOKS